The Joy Molecule

C$_2$P

How to Unlock the Power of Human Connection

LARRY KESSLIN

The Joy Molecule: How to Unlock the Power of Human
Connection
by Larry Kesslin

Published by

 HUMAN
CONNECTION
PRESS

For information, contact: Larry@LarryKesslin.com

Book Design: Nick Zelinger, NZGraphics.com
Developmental Editing: Judith Briles, The Book Shepherd
Line Editing: Peggy Ireland

ISBN: 979-8-9998274-0-1 (Print)
ISBN: 979-8-9998274-1-8 (Ebook)
ISBN: 979-8-9998274-2-5 (Audiobook)
LCCN: 2025917474

First Edition

Printed in the United States of America

Contents

Author's Note

My life has been beautiful, if only I had experienced it that way. I have had so many amazing moments; however, I was so incomplete and alone along the way that I never noticed.

In 1993, I spent a week with 85 inner-city kids in a program called Grass Roots Aspen Experience held in Aspen, Colorado. That volunteer trip taught me one of the most important lessons of my life: being happy and feeling joy had nothing to do with my situation in life. I was 29 years old, and I was empty. I was blaming everyone else for my problems. From the outside, it might have looked like I was living the dream, but in reality, I was miserable.

The next 20 years were focused on making money, finding a life partner to build a family, volunteering, and looking to make an impact, and that was it.

In 1998, I got married, and two years later, children came into my life. We seemed like a happy little family unit with two adorable and well-behaved children, and we were. The only challenge was the yearning that was inside of me the whole time. I never felt complete. I was always looking for something outside of me to make me feel better.

In 2010, we took a leap and moved from New York to San Diego, California. In San Diego, I enjoyed being outside all the time. I was able to play all the sports that I had ever wanted to play. And I had found peace. But most importantly, I had found my tribe in California.

On July 23, 2012 my family and I flew from JFK Airport to Istanbul, and then from Istanbul to Entebbe, Uganda. The next 24 days would change the course of my life forever. Everyone was talking about purpose and the need to find a meaningful life. That trip was a pivotal time for me on so many levels. I saw people who were incredibly happy and full of joy, but I kept using the hammer of purpose with everyone I met. I thought purpose was one's ultimate destination.

I spent the next 18 months trying to figure out what I had experienced in Uganda and Kenya. I met with dozens of friends to dissect my thoughts and was able to deliver a TEDx Talk in January of 2014 called The Disconnected, Connected World. The past decade-plus I have been living out these concepts and learning about what brings me joy.

The Joy Molecule is a culmination of numerous lessons that I've learned over the past six decades. Joy is rooted in deep human connection, and this book is about my journey to that vision of joy. The stories shared here are from a few of the beautiful souls that I've met who have been my greatest teachers. On this journey, I have learned to love myself, love my life, and find peace. This peace is so deep and so clear that at times I can taste it.

Within these pages, I tell stories about some special individuals who have taught me the most valuable lessons of my life.

They became the lightning rod for me to see a path to joy and to learn what makes up *The Joy Molecule*.

I hope that these stories might move you as you progress on your unique journey.

To a life lived with JOY,

1

The Power of Joy

Is it possible that the unconscious mind controls everything, and has access to all awareness?

Everyone is brought into this world in a moment. You come out from this warm place inside your mother's womb, and when you hit the cold air of reality, you let out a big scream.

Hello World, I'm here!

You arrive on this planet unaware of many things. Things like:

- Why am I here?
- What am I supposed to do on this upcoming journey?
- Why did I get the parents I got?
- How will I manage what's to come?

I have been gifted with over six decades of life thus far, and what I know at this point is that I know nothing, absolutely nothing! The question I'm addressing here is what is knowledge? What do we truly know?

What I do have is a lot of ideas and beliefs about what this journey is all about, and this book is designed for you to see a possible explanation that might bring some joy to your life. I've traveled around the world; built a successful business; visited 48 of the 50 states; and ridden a bike from San Francisco to San Diego; and so much more.

In the end, I believe that you are here to live out the meaning of your soul's unique journey.

Each person is made up of three different parts. The first part is a physical body that carries two other entities. These two entities are closely linked yet separate: our mind and our soul.

For most of my life, I had little to no direct access to my soul. Instead, it's been my mind that has been running the show— totally. That is, until I went on a few journeys that changed everything: My outlook, my business, and me.

Yet this book is not about me ... rather my journey of learning from others. It's not about what I know. It's about the possibilities. My experiences have revealed that people do seek joy. They want to feel joy and feel it all the time. The problem is that they are running in the wrong direction to embrace it.

The Joy Molecule is designed to provide one person's perspective on the word joy and what it means. It is not only how I found joy, but it's about how it is enhanced when shared with others on a deep, meaningful level. I will disclose how I came across this belief system and how you might be able to access more joy in your life.

The challenge is that my mind doesn't want the same thing my soul does. The mind is where my ego lives, where my identity lives, and where I form all my interpretations of this world.

Multiple studies have stated that you might have access to 10% of what is going on in your brain, which is the conscious mind. The other 90% of what is going on in your brain is the unconscious mind.

- Is it possible that the unconscious mind controls everything, has access to all awareness?

- Is it possible that the 10% that you have access to is there just to mess with you?

- Is it possible that your unconscious mind knows exactly what your soul needs?

- Is it possible that when you release your mind to do what it does best, create thoughts, then life will be so much simpler?

Let's talk about this idea that your mind creates thoughts.

I have been meditating for the last 15 years. And I've been dedicated to my practice with a group that has met every weekday morning for the past five years. This practice has gotten deeper over the past year, and I am realizing how many thoughts my mind creates and learning what to do with them.

What I've learned is that they are just thoughts. I don't need to do anything with them. The problem humans have is in believing those thoughts are real and that they are one's life. I used to believe that, but thoughts are just suggestions. You get to decide which ones you listen to and which ones you say no to. This thing called the mind can keep you from accessing your inner self—your soul.

In addition to your thoughts, you also experience feelings. Feelings are also suggestions on what to do. Do you need to react to them? Maybe … maybe not.

Combine these thoughts and feelings, and that is what runs most lives. Now take a step back and see these thoughts and feelings for what they are. Merely information that you get to choose how to interpret. When you do, you will find more peace and allow your soul, or subconscious, to run the show.

Many refer to this as *living in the flow*. Think of this as being focused and fully immersed in what you are doing and surrounded by enjoyment as you do it. I believe that finding a way to have one's soul and one's own mind work in concert to manage this vehicle called a body is the path for me, a path that keeps my joy molecule engaged.

I have been involved in dozens of personal development workshops. One I'm currently involved with is a program called Insight, originally designed by John Roger. The program reveals three levels of self: the *basic self,* the *conscious self,* and the *higher self.* This construct makes sense to me at this point in my journey.

The basic self is you acting like you are a five- or six-year-old child. It is extremely reactionary and keeps you from being present. Many call this the *inner child.* This inner child reacts to every thought and every feeling that comes forward.

There are two sides to the basic self: the playful child and the child that is in pain. Keeping that inner child alive is critically important, and acknowledging its presence is extremely healthy for me. I love the playful child in me, and I've learned that it's the pain associated with my inner child that can wreak havoc in my life.

The conscious self is the part of you that lives your age. At this moment, I have a level of awareness that can allow me to act versus react and take responsibility for my actions. I know that my basic self blames everyone else for my problems, but my conscious self takes personal responsibility. It does not blame others and lives close to the principles in Don Miguel Ruiz's *The Four Agreements.*

The higher self is this sense of knowing, this belief that everything is unfolding perfectly. It's the stuff that Michael Singer wrote about in *The Untethered Soul,* about living life freely and realizing that we are insignificant.

For most of my life, I have lived as my basic self, with moments of my conscious self showing up. I have been extremely ego-driven, looking to defend my position and believed that what I believed was right and everyone needed to hear it. I was begging for attention; I was acting like the 5-year-old boy who didn't get his way. I was screaming to be heard.

I was alone, I was hurting, and I didn't know how to handle it. I would go into episodes of deep depression, and I wanted someone to save me.

That was the 5-year-old boy begging for someone ... anyone ... to come to the rescue. My conscious self has learned that the only one who can save me ... is me!

The power of joy

I'm involved with an organization in San Diego called Boys to Men Mentoring (B2M). B2M is an amazing organization that helps teen boys transition to manhood. The basic principles are rooted in the concept that, as a child, it is common to blame others for problems. To become a man, the participant needs to take responsibility for his situation in life and own them and not blame anyone else.

The program also focuses on the four archetypes of a man: king, warrior, lover, and magician. These two constructs shape the program: stop blaming others for anything and understand what it means to be a man. I have been participating in programs with B2M for several years and continue to learn more from the boys than I teach them.

In every situation where I've been of service to others, I have always received so much more than what I gave. It is the power of joy.

So how does this all relate to joy?

- How does understanding that individuals have three separate parts: the mind produces thoughts; the body feels; and the soul is the ultimate guide?

- What is so important about knowing about your Basic Self, your Conscious Self and your Higher Self?

These concepts are critical if you are to find joy in life. Building constructs that make sense to me help explain why life shows up the way it does.

I learned early in my life that if I defined things, it was much easier to attain them. Therefore, it's critical to have a definition for any word if you are going to try to attain it.

As an extreme extrovert, I have met thousands of people in my life. I have asked many of them to share their definition of happiness and joy. It is difficult to describe a feeling if you have no personal definition for it. How will you know if you are happy or joyful if neither word is defined in your mind … in your experience?

I wrote my definition of success when I was 28 and rewrote that definition 20 years later, when the first definition did not work for me any longer. That was the foundation for my last book, *Success Redefined.* Now, I get to play with happiness and joy because I believe they are incredibly connected, yet there is a difference between the two words.

The standard definition of *happiness* for most is: involving positive emotions and life satisfaction.

Today, my definition of happiness is simply this: *getting your needs met.*

In *Success Redefined,* I covered this topic in detail. The challenge that comes with that definition is understanding the difference between a want and a need. What is a want and what is a need? I have a 23-year-old son who grew up saying "Daddy, I need this and Daddy, I need that …." If you met my son Noah, he would tell you that we've had more conversations about wants vs needs than any other topic of conversation. I believe the less you need, the easier it is to be happy.

Joy is a knowing …

So, what about joy?

I was not raised with joy in my life. It is something that I've needed to seek and learn about. I meet many people who are filled with joy, and some of them have had it their whole life. What is it about these people that brings them joy and allows them to live what seems like an effortless life?

The standard definition of *joy* for most is: a feeling of great pleasure and happiness.

I have searched for joy since I could think and feel.

What does joy feel like?
What does it taste like to be joyful?
What does joy look like?

Asking and probing these questions, I finally came to my definition of joy:

Joy is a knowing ...
knowing What you are, Who you are,
and Why you are here.

This book is my opportunity to explain this definition. I'm not saying I'm right, and I'm not saying I know anything. What I'm trying to do is get what's in my head out on paper and see if it resonates with others. I had a conversation recently with my brother Ken, and he asked me to please write my next book for myself and not try to push my thoughts onto others. So, thank you, Ken, for being the wise older brother and suggesting I write from a different perspective. This book is an opportunity for me to share some thoughts that I hope will resonate with you. And I hope it might help you find more happiness, peace, and joy.

2

The Joy Molecule

Your *What, Who,* and *Why* form the energetic orbit around your truest self.

What if joy isn't something you chase, but something you remember—by simply knowing what you are, who you are, and why you are here?

My working definition for joy is this:

Knowing What you are, Who you are, and Why you are here.

To understand the elements of joy, it's essential to break down the *What, Who,* and *Why.*

What You Are

Your **What** is the tangible expression of your skills, talents, and actions—the roles you play, the hats you wear, the things you create or accomplish.

- It's your contribution to the world through your work, craft, hobbies, and responsibilities.

- It can change many times over a lifetime, but it's often what people first see or name when they describe you.

Who You Are

Your **Who** is your character, your essence, your way of being. It's the emotional and relational fabric of your presence.

- It's how you show up when titles and roles are stripped away.

- It includes your values, personality traits, emotional patterns, and the energy you carry into a room.

- It's the part of you that knows when something is unfair.

- It's the human experience of you; what others feel from being around you.

Why You Are Here

Your **Why** is your soul's purpose; your deepest reason for being that transcends roles, achievements, and expectations.

- It's the inner call that lights you up and gives your life direction.

- It's not what you do or how you act; it's why it all matters.

- When shared with others, it creates the deepest, most fulfilling connections.

Together, your What, Who, and Why form the energetic orbit around your truest self. And when you live with this self-awareness and connect with others who are also living on purpose, you ignite something greater.

In my last book, I shared this simple equation:

Conscious Connection + Purpose = Joy

Condensed, it becomes C_2P = **Joy.**

Just as H_2O is the chemical formula for water, **what if C_2P is the molecule for joy?**

At that moment, **The Joy Molecule** was born.

In this molecule, JOY is the central atom, surrounded by three other atoms:

Your What, your Who, and your Why.

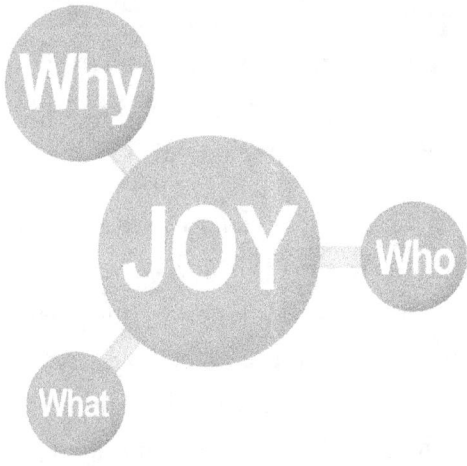

At the start of this book, I stated that joy is rooted in deep human connection. When you look at levels of connection, a **What** connection is where most conversations begin. You find commonality through what you do, the sports you play, and the hobbies that you pursue. These connections are great, yet they lack the depth of getting beyond the surface.

When you probe deeper, you may connect around your **Who,** your values and personalities.

It is these relationships that started to intrigue me as my life evolved. But it's the **Why** connection that brings the most joy to my life.

As I've learned what is important to me, I started to steer conversations away from the *What* and started to lean into the *Who* and eventually focused primarily on the *Why*. When I leaned into the Who and the Why, many people wanted to go back to the What conversation. The more conscious I have become about this insight, the more I knew that this person—one who focused on the what—wasn't someone I wanted to spend a lot of time with. They are not bad people; they are just not my tribe.

The stories in *The Joy Module* are about individuals who connected with me at a Why level—people whose purpose resonated with mine. These connections helped me see myself more clearly and reminded me of what truly matters. I invite you into the stories ahead. May you see yourself not just in my journey, but in your own unfolding path to joy.

3

Circumstance Does Not Define You

I have no idea ... but not this!

My journey to joy first began when I was 29 years old. I was working at General Electric (GE), the #1 company in the world at the time, and I felt empty. Then I was told about an organization that was taking young people from across the US to Aspen, Colorado.

I chaperoned 12 young males, ages ranging from 15 to 17. They came from the Henry Street Settlement on the Lower East Side of Manhattan in New York. Along with 70-plus others, we spent a week teaching these boys to ski. On the last night of the trip, I was standing in a dark hallway. Shivering from the cold, I could see the fog of my breath fill the air. While in the auditorium there were some 80 teens celebrating. They had just completed a week of skiing, and they were having the time of their life!

As I stood in the hallway, I wondered, *What was I doing?* How was this college-educated engineer (me), with an amazing career trajectory, not happy? It was at that moment that I realized happiness had nothing to do with my circumstances.

I returned from that ski trip on February 28, and two days later I quit my job. My boss asked me, "What are you going to do?"

I told him, "I have no idea … but not this!"

This was the start of my entrepreneurial journey.

Over the next 20 years, I learned how to become a successful entrepreneur; a good husband and father; and a productive member of society. I cared about making a difference and leaving this planet better than I found it.

In the fall of 2011, I met a woman who was taking computers to rural villages in Africa. We started talking and I was enthralled. In fact, I was so excited about this endeavor that I joined the board of U-TOUCH, a San Diego-based non-profit that focused its work in rural Ugandan villages. My family and I decided to go to Uganda that following summer to check out the program.

That trip changed my life forever.

It was 3:55 a.m. on Sunday, July 29, 2012, when we arrived at Entebbe International Airport, the only international airport in Uganda. As my wife, son, daughter, and I approached the carousel to locate our suitcases, I heard someone mention a list at the far corner of the room. We were looking for our bags, but none had come down the conveyor.

I decided to go and check out "the list." The first four names on the list were Kesslin, Kesslin, Kesslin, and Kesslin. The plane was overweight, and Turkish Airlines needed to leave some bags behind in Istanbul. OMG, none of our bags had made it to Uganda. We would need to survive with only the contents of our carry-ons until the suitcases arrived.

A driver was waiting for us at the airport. I thought I had conveyed our desire to make it to Kampala safely, saying that we were in no rush. Unfortunately, the driver spoke only a few words of English. As a British colony, Ugandans drive on the opposite side of the road, which is unnerving for American drivers—even as passengers. I sat in the passenger seat and my wife and kids sat in the back. Our driver turned into Mario Andretti, doing crazy fast maneuvering, racing around corners, passing other cars on turns, with cows, people, bicycles, and more on the side of the road. And all of this dangerous driving was happening while it was black outside.

That taxi ride from Entebbe Airport to Kampala was one of the most horrific and terrifying experiences of my life. And I promised, after arriving safely at our new friend's home in Kampala, that we would never get back in a taxi when it was dark in Uganda. It was a frightening experience that none of us wanted to relive.

Boy, did we exceed our expectations on so many levels!

Being a regular traveler, you would think that I would have made sure that my family had some items in their carry-on if something like this happened. This was not the case. We had very few extra clothes, with our toiletries in our large bags to avoid dealing with security restrictions. It was a rough beginning in regard to our suitcases, but it would turn out to be an amazing journey that we took over the next week. It took Turkish Airlines six days to locate and deliver our bags.

We would be staying in the home of a nonprofit leader in Kampala, Joshua Kyallo, for the first couple of days. And fortunately for us, his family had ample clothes for all of us, even if my clothes were a bit snug, maybe a size too small. Maybe there was a message for me to lose a few pounds.

Joshua was the CEO of AMREF, an international nonprofit that dealt with health issues in multiple African countries. AMREF was the organization that had partnered with U-TOUCH to host the computer labs in their facilities. As a board member of U-TOUCH, I wanted to experience the work firsthand and expose our 10- and 12-year-old children to a different world. Boy, did we exceed our expectations on so many levels!

The Suitcase Saga Begins

Two days after our arrival, my wife and I met with a young male Turkish Airlines representative who said we would be given $600 to help us purchase items since our bags had been detained in Istanbul. However, about 10 minutes later, he returned and corrected himself, saying that he could only give us $300 for our inconvenience. At this point, we were a bit agitated. I asked to speak with the person in charge to discuss the issue.

Minutes later, we were sitting in front of the country director for Turkish Airlines. The director was pleasant but firm in what he could do for us. He said our bags would be at the airport the next morning and that he would deliver them upon arrival.

My wife was angry. She continued to insist that we get more than the $300 offered, but the director of the airlines was not budging. He explained that he could not offer more as it had been less than 72 hours since our arrival. He was only authorized to provide us compensation for one lost bag, which was $300.

Of course, this director had not lost our bags. He was just following the company guidelines. I accepted the monetary exchange and asked him when we could expect our bags to arrive. They were scheduled to be on a plane leaving Istanbul that evening and would arrive early the next morning. I declined the offer to deliver our bags.

Going to pick up our bags the next morning meant that I was back to driving in the dark, except this time I knew the driver and he spoke good English. It wasn't nearly as scary as our first taxi ride. Our bags would be on the same flight we had arrived on at 3:45 a.m. a few days earlier.

Now back at the airport, we saw the young man who had originally promised us the $600. We said hello but he ran past quickly, without acknowledging us. We should have known something was wrong. When we got to the baggage carousel, we were told that our bags had not made it on that flight. Three hours of driving and no luggage to collect!

We returned to Kampala and as soon as the Turkish Airlines office opened, I took a taxi with Joshua, our new local friend, to visit the country director of Turkish Airlines once again. As before, I was calm and polite, and the director was very apologetic. It wasn't his fault; after all, he was just the one delivering the bad news.

Joshua was extremely animated, telling the man why we were in Uganda, about the work we were doing to help the people of Uganda gain access to the greatest library in the world: the

Ugandan roads are typically called an African Massage.

internet. At this point, the director did not hesitate in handing me another $900 in cash: all the money he was allowed to offer individuals for losing their bags, bringing our total compensation to $1,200.

Since Joshua had clothes for all of us, we only had to spend $200 on toiletries and a few pharmacy items. Again, we were promised that our bags would be on the next plane, which was not scheduled to arrive for a few more days.

Finally, Our Journey Begins

We decided to get in our van and head east to begin our journey. We spent an afternoon in Jinja on Thursday and arrived in Mbale on Friday, a small town in eastern Uganda, close to the Kenyan border.

Finally, our luggage arrived on Friday morning in Entebbe, an eight-hour drive from Mbale. Turkish Airlines arranged and paid for the transport to bring us our bags.

We collected our bags and exited the main area of town, driving on dirt roads toward the Abayudaya community. If you have never driven in a country like Uganda, it is an experience. These roads are typically referred to as an African Massage. As you drive, the divots in the road cause the car to bounce up and down, left and right, it feels like you're going to get whiplash! We stayed on this road for a few miles until we reached our destination, a small village with a few dozen people and a beautiful modern building. We had arrived at the Abayudaya community.

The Abayudaya is a community of more than 500 Jews who live in eastern Uganda and have for many generations. It is believed that there are approximately 1,500 Jews in Uganda, with the Abayudaya as the largest group in one place in the country. We started to find our way around this amazing place and got settled into our accommodation for the next three nights. We walked down to the school that was a half mile away. The school did not resemble any school that we had ever seen before. The buildings were all painted white, and on the walls outside were maps, equations, and positive affirmations. There were not many textbooks at the school, so most of the major lessons were painted on the building.

It was amazing.

Meet Armstrong

Upon our return from our walk, Debra, the woman who invited us on this amazing trip, told us about a young man known as Armstrong. She mentioned that she had known him for five years and he was the smartest person she had met since she started visiting Uganda seven years ago. She told us that Armstrong had always dreamt of becoming an airline pilot and that he needed $1,000 to take a pilot's test.

I was intrigued and learned that he lived in Nairobi, near Wilson Airport, the puddle jumper airport that took travelers to safaris all around Kenya. Armstrong had a small tent that he lived in on a friend's property about 20 minutes from the airport. He worked each day doing whatever he could to make one or two dollars a day. He would wash airplanes, carry bags or do anything he could to earn enough to purchase a bottle of water and a piece of bread. He was smart and very determined to achieve his dream of being a pilot.

I was introduced to Armstrong that first evening and was struck by his wisdom at such a young age. He was 24 years old and had already experienced so much in his life. He shared his interpretations of the Bible and how the community had shaped his life. He walked many miles each day to get from place to place and was extremely humble.

While we were getting to know him on that first day, Armstrong shared a story that was amazing. When he was 16 years old, he had made one of the boldest decisions I had ever heard of. He left his home with a singular goal: to get to Israel.

Armstrong grew up in a small village in Uganda. His parents were loving and worked hard to give their kids a good life. One day, when Armstrong was nine, he saw a wooden menorah in his house. That moment sparked something in him. He started reading about Israel and the Jewish people. He became fascinated by their history, their struggles, and how they always seemed to rise again. Over the next few years, that spark grew into something bigger. It became his purpose.

At sixteen, he got a passport by saying he was eighteen and headed out on his own with only $300. He hid a map in his sock and quietly left Uganda. His journey lasted fourteen months. It was filled with danger, kindness from strangers, and moments that changed him forever.

He traveled through Kenya, then Somalia, where he was arrested. While in custody, a Somali leader saw something special in him and made him an offer: teach my kids English and I will help you continue your journey. Armstrong stayed for a few months and learned how to drive, fix weapons, and survive in a tough place. They even offered him cows and a wife to stay, but he said no. He wasn't meant to stay; he had to continue on his trek.

He kept walking through Ethiopia, Sudan, Egypt, getting closer to his dream. He followed the same path the Israelites once walked. He slept in the desert, crossed rivers, and faced border guards with nothing but courage and a dream.

Finally, he made it to the border of Israel. He was the only Black person among thousands of Palestinians. He felt different but not scared. He had come so far.

But then the gate closed. They wouldn't let him in. No reason. No explanation. Just no.

Armstrong didn't break down. He didn't give up. He was sent back to Cairo and the Egyptians put him on an airplane back to Entebbe. He returned to Uganda with no money, no food, and no way to call his family. Out of options, he walked home and knocked on his family's door.

His sister fainted when she saw him. His parents were in shock. For days, no one said anything. They couldn't believe he was alive.

But the failure of not getting into Israel didn't stop Armstrong. He went back to school, became one of the first people in his town to learn how to use a computer, studied aviation, and eventually found himself at Wilson Airport in Nairobi.

As I listened to Armstrong's story, it was obvious that he was a deeply thoughtful human being and his passion for becoming a pilot was evident.

Remember, we had just been handed $1,200 by an airline for losing our bags. I've met so many who regularly travel that never get anything for a lost bag, yet we were very generously compensated. After meeting Armstrong, I had to share his story with my wife and kids. I told them that I would like to give the money we got from the airline to Armstrong. We had created a budget for the trip and the compensation from Turkish Airlines was unexpected, and it would not materially change our lives. As I spoke of the impression young Armstrong had made upon me, I added that we were in a position that could totally change his life. My wife agreed to meet with Armstrong the following morning to see for herself what he was all about.

Before traveling to Uganda, we were told to bring $100 bills by our travel coordinator, and all bills were to be newer than 2008. I spent several days before our trip going to different banks to make sure that all of our money was dated 2009 or later. On that Saturday morning, I removed ten crisp $100 bills from my computer bag and handed them to Armstrong. His eyes expanded in front of us. Armstrong was speechless.

That meeting created a relationship that lives to this day. We could never have imagined what a ride we had just begun.

Prior to our trip to Uganda, U-TOUCH had placed a container on a ship with 150 computers donated by a biotech firm in San Diego. Thirty of the computers were eventually used to open a computer center in the library that was at the center of the Abayudaya community.

• • • • •

Leaving the Abayudaya, we spent over a week visiting other sites around Uganda, including Gulu, the northern most established city on the way to Sudan. Upon completing our time in Uganda, we flew to Kenya and went on a safari in Amboseli National Park and the Masai Mara. What an amazing experience we had, and one that will live with me forever.

We got to see some of the world's most amazing natural attractions, including hundreds of thousands of wildebeests, zebras, lions, cheetahs, vultures, rhinos, and giraffes.

In Amboseli, we witnessed the great elephant parade. Each day the elephants walk from the forest to the marsh and each evening, they make the return trip. In the Masai, we witnessed the Great Migration and were fortunate enough to see two crossings of the Masai River by a pack of wildebeests and zebras. We saw

Mr. Larry ... now I need money for flight lessons.

crocodiles swimming in the same waters. It was truly nature at its finest. My family was in awe.

After completing our safari adventure, we landed at Wilson Airport in Nairobi. As we gathered our bags, in the distance

I hear someone yelling, "Mr. Larry, Mr. Larry!" Armstrong was walking toward us with a huge smile on his face and the first words out of his mouth were, "I passed the test!" I was so proud of him and excited that we had contributed a small piece to this young man's future. As soon as he told me that he had passed, he then said, "Mr. Larry … now I need money for flight lessons."

His words surprised me. I had just returned from an amazing week and was not yet ready to discuss funding this young man's future. I told Armstrong, "I'm leaving for home tomorrow, I am in no condition to have this conversation right now. I will call you after I return home."

The following Sunday I called Armstrong's cell phone, and we discussed possible next steps. We had a nice conversation and then he shared, "I need $7,000 to take classes to get my private pilot's license." He told me that he had a job offer waiting for him with Tanzania Air if he completed his training. Armstrong was very sure of himself. I could feel his excitement about the opportunity to become a pilot through our phone connection.

At this point, my business was doing extremely well. We were raising two young children and had everything that we needed, and then some. We were able to travel, put our kids in any sports programs that they wanted, attend any events that we wanted, and enjoy our amazing life in San Diego. But something was still missing for me. I felt it daily. What was it?

Over the next decade, I would experience a personal transformation that would teach me one of the biggest lessons in my life.

The lesson? It was the essential lesson of giving … to learn to become part of something greater than oneself. Armstrong was my first significant journey along this path. I had always volunteered and wanted to be of service, yet this felt different.

I decided to wire Armstrong $7,500 the following week. It turns out that Armstrong's command of the English language was not very strong. I told him that $7,000 was for the flight lessons and $500 was for an English tutor. Sunday morning became our time to talk. I began to talk with Armstrong every other Sunday morning. I would play volleyball on the beach each Sunday at 8 a.m. PST in San Diego, and I would get up early and call Armstrong at 7 a.m. PST, which was 5 p.m. in Nairobi. Each time we spoke, we would discuss his training and what he needed. Over the coming months, Armstrong's English improved greatly with the help of his English tutor. And he completed his private pilot training.

Upon the completion of his training, he went to meet with a man he called "The Admiral." The Admiral worked at Tanzania

It was at this point that I realized that I was in over my head.

Air and had promised Armstrong a job as a pilot if he could complete his training. Armstrong was very good at meeting influential individuals in his life, and The Admiral was another person who wanted to see him succeed. On one of our Sunday calls, I could tell that Armstrong was extremely hesitant and didn't want to share something with me. I probed deeper and Armstrong finally shared his news. Upon meeting with The Admiral and showing him the private pilot's certificate, Armstrong was told that he needed a commercial pilot's license, not a private pilot's license. This would require an additional $50,000 investment. It was at this point that I realized that I was in over my head.

In my desire to make an impact in the world, I had started to network with other purpose-driven change makers. One of them owned a company called Digital Data Divide. DDD trained young people in third world countries to use computers to do low level tasks. The training was powerful and the work was plentiful. DDD would engage large corporations that had low level tech work that needed to be completed and DDD would fulfill on those needs.

It just so happened that the Chief Operating Officer (COO) of DDD, Kirunda Kiruthi, was stationed in Nairobi. We had become friends, and the most amazing thing is that as well as being the COO of DDD, he was a licensed commercial airline pilot! After learning of his experience, I asked him if he would meet with Armstrong and let me know if this young man was worth continuing to invest in. I am not a pilot and have no idea what it takes to become one, so I needed an outside opinion.

Over the next month, Armstrong met with Kirunda and the message was very positive. Armstrong was the type of person that would make an excellent pilot and had what it took to complete the training. It was very clear to me that there was no way that I could afford to pay for his training, so I had an idea. If I could get Armstrong to the US, I had lots of smart and wealthy friends that would help me fund his training.

That following week on our call, I told Armstrong that if he could get a visa to the US, we would find a way to make this happen. Armstrong spent the next seven months doing everything in his power to prepare to meet with the US Embassy to attain a visa. His first visit to the Embassy was on January 7, 2014. He met with a visa agent and the first question she asked was, "Why do you want to go to the US?"

Armstrong was ready with his answer. "I want to learn to become a pilot so I can come back home and change my country." After a few more questions, in what seemed like a dream to Armstrong, the woman behind the counter approved his visa application on the first visit. To say this is unusual is an understatement. His prayers had been answered!

With this news, I immediately purchased a one-way plane ticket to San Diego, and on February 6, 2014, Armstrong's journey to the US began. I met him at the at the San Diego International Airport. His face was exuberant and we embraced in greeting. Once we collected his bags, we headed to the parking lot. Armstrong had never been in

When I walked in, I saw the shock on Armstrong's face.

a car like mine. One of my criteria for leaving New York was to find a place to live where I could drive a convertible 12 months a year.

When we exited the airport, we jumped on the 5 highway and headed toward Carlsbad. Armstrong's jaw dropped in amazement. We were on a 10-lane highway, driving at 75 mph with the top down. There were no potholes, no massive traffic jams, the weather was beautiful, and we had wide open space to cruise to our destination.

The weekend that Armstrong arrived was when my mother-in-law was staying at our home. With our guest bedroom occupied, I dropped Armstrong at a friend's house less than a half mile from our home. It was later in the evening, so I told Armstrong to get some sleep, and I would be back in the morning to pick him up.

Upon waking, I called my friend and headed over to collect Armstrong and his things. When I walked in, I saw the shock on Armstrong's face. He was walking around this home, not believing what he was seeing. He had never seen clean sheetrock walls, recessed lighting, and wall switches that controlled everything. After my wife's mother left, I drove Armstrong to our home. He walked around with the same amazement as he had displayed earlier that morning. Then he asked me if there was a place where he could build a fire. When I asked him why he needed to build a fire, he stated that he wanted to make some hot tea. It was at this moment that I realized that Armstrong was in for a culture shock of epic proportions.

Realizing that he was in a new world, I said, "Come with me." For the next 30 minutes, I showed him the water cooler in our kitchen and poured some boiling hot water for tea. I showed him our appliances: dishwasher, refrigerator, and washer/dryer.

After pushing the little red tab on the water cooler and getting hot water, Armstrong had looked behind the machine and asked, "Where is the fire?" He was so innocent for so many reasons, and now he had a chance to experience how another part of the world lived.

This was just the beginning of an amazing journey that has been our life together over the past decade. From the beginning, I was Mr. Larry.

Armstrong met a wonderful young woman, Melinda, back in early 2020 and in June of that year we hosted a small wedding in our backyard in Carlsbad to wed the two. Later that year, we welcomed baby Gray. Armstrong is building a wonderfully loving family. Armstrong has been through flight training, with 300+ hours of flight and has earned a private pilot's license in the US. He realized that his skills were better at fixing the planes as much, if not more, than flying them. He received his certificate in airframe and engine maintenance in 2019 and 2020. He started working for an international company, maintaining UPS systems with a focus on helping small airlines with maintenance work.

When we first started investing in Armstrong, we were very clear. We were not investing in his life to help him become an American. We were investing in him to get the training he needed and to go back to his country so that he could make an impact. Now that he has established a life and career, it is time to return home.

Some opportunities have presented themselves over the past few years, including the opportunity to invest in a hangar at Wilson Airport in Nairobi. It turns out that the hangar that Armstrong spent most of his time at in Nairobi was owned by an Italian couple. In 2017, the Italian man who owned it had passed away. His wife had been looking for Armstrong for two years, hoping that he would come back and take over the hangar operations.

In 2019 it was some five years since Armstrong had been back to Nairobi. The hangar was old and **Armstrong is now part of my family.** needed repair. Three planes still resided in the hangar but had not been flown in decades. A couple of years ago, Armstrong found a buyer for one of the planes and the proceeds from that sale allowed him to purchase a larger share of the hangar.

Back in 2012, this all seemed like a dream to a young man who yearned to become a commercial airline pilot. Armstrong is now part of my family. And in many ways, the story has only just begun. We expect Armstrong to return to Sub-Saharan Africa (Uganda & Kenya) with his wife, Melinda, and boys Gray and Armstrong. They are a wonderful young family and have such a bright future ahead of them.

I know that I will find my way back to Uganda and Kenya at some point, especially as we will have family there. The depth of passion that Armstrong has for life, and his desire to connect with the deepest version of himself, is so inspiring for me and everyone that meets him. When you combine passion, hard work, and focus on a dream, amazing things can happen.

Lessons I Learned from Armstrong ...

Armstrong is a role model of perseverance and motivation that is not common, and one that I wish to emulate in my life every day. He has taught me that our situation in life does not define our happiness or our joy. He has seen so much hardship, and he still walks with a sense of confidence and peace. Armstrong knows what he is ... who he is ... and why he is here. He approaches every day with wonder and opportunity with a smile on his face. Daily, he pushes forward.

We all have challenges in our life, yet when Armstrong gets challenged, he finds a way.

Thank you, Armstrong, for knowing what you are, who you are, and why you are here.

4

Redirecting Capital

How do I donate $1,000,000 to the Global Good Fund?

We left Nairobi on August 17, 2012, and arrived in New York City 30 hours later. I was smelly and definitely in need of a shower. We had a multi-hour layover before our flight back to San Diego and I started to think, what did I just experience? I saw so many people, not just Armstrong, that walked on this planet with happiness and joy. Yet, they had so much less than I did. Why were they so much happier than I was?

My life was great; this is true. I had the house, the cars, the beautiful kids, and I was living in San Diego. So, what could be wrong? But what I was seeking was a deeper sense of happiness and contentment. What I was seeking is what Michael Singer refers to as inner peace in his books, *The Untethered Soul* and *Living Untethered.*

Seven weeks later, I was on a plane to Ixtapa, Mexico, to attend Opportunity Collaboration (OC). OC is known as the "Unconference." The only speakers were the participants, and there were over 400 of us! We were all there to learn about solving world poverty. This was my first time at an OC event. Each year that I attended became a unique experience. I attended OC in 2012, 2013, 2014 and 2024. The OC programs that I have attended have had a strong influence on me, but my family's trip to Uganda in 2012 has had the most significant impact on my life.

Upon returning from Uganda, I started questioning everything.

It was my first day at OC in 2012, and I was in a small group of 15 people, called a colloquium. We would meet together every morning of the conference to discuss poverty and our roles in effecting this issue. The facilitator started the first morning by writing three questions on a flip chart. The three questions were:

What is poverty?
Who gets to define it?
Why are we trying to fix it?

It was at that moment that my mind felt like it was going to explode! I had just returned from a country that most people would call poor to extremely poor, and I had witnessed happiness and joy. With my experience and observations, I now asked myself:

What is poverty?

Is it possible that the people I met in Uganda were not poor at all; they were just impoverished?

Is the US poor, especially when it comes to the topics of happiness and joy?

Why are we, in the US, always the ones trying to fix the rest of the world?

Do we need them to be more like us for us to feel happy?

Upon returning from Uganda, I started questioning everything. My African experience showed me that happiness and joy can be totally independent from our situation in life. Why were the Ugandans joyful, people who had so little, while so many people around me in the US were stressed, unhappy, and disconnected? What was going on?

Maybe the problem isn't poverty, but it's perception. The real issue isn't that we in the US don't have enough, but that we don't know what "enough" is.

The 20 Something Rule

I've had this philosophy for the past decade and I've been sharing it with people, and it has resonated with many. When you are born, the world around you is influential on many levels. The world, mostly your immediate family for the very early years, is showing you who you should be; how you should act; and what you should like and dislike. It is based on your training as a human being and what the world around you wants you to be.

As a young person, you are influenced by everything around you: your peers, teachers, movies, the media, Madison Avenue, Hollywood, and more. That is until "that day" comes. That day, for some, is somewhere around 20 years old, when a voice enters your head and says, "Do I want to be the person that the world told me to be, or do I want to become the person I was born to be?"

Many go to their grave never answering this question, and they end up living their lives based on what they were taught or told as a child. And many have never had that thought.

I believe that somewhere around one in one thousand people are taught by their surroundings to be the person that they were born to be. That means that the rest of us schmucks need to shed the faux identity and figure out who we were meant to be. I suspect that this could be you too.

Meet Carrie Rich

At OC in 2013, I met a young woman who has become one of my dearest friends. I wish I could spend more time with her, yet she is super busy and lives on the other side of the country. Her name is Carrie Rich, and she is the ONE in ONE THOUSAND that was taught to be the person she was born to be. Carrie was 27 years old when I met her, and she was amazing. She has always known what she is, who she is, and why she is here.

Redirecting Capital

A few days before Carrie Rich's 26th birthday, her boss, Knox Johnson, handed her an envelope containing one hundred dollars. Carrie was working at INOVA, a large healthcare company based in northern Virginia. Mr. Johnson told her that he could take her out to lunch to celebrate her birthday or give her birthday money so she could do something good with it. This simple act of kindness was the beginning of a journey that would change both of their lives.

Carrie was an extremely high performer, already a Director at INOVA at a young age after graduating from business school at Georgetown. She was passionate about her work and about making an impact in the world. She was reporting directly to the CEO of the company and was on track to becoming the CEO of a growing company at some point in the next decade, until her journey took a significant turn.

After receiving the envelope containing $100 from her boss, Carrie decided that she would like to do more. She wanted to expand the giving and crafted an email that she would soon send out to everyone that she knew. The subject line of the email was: The Global Good Fund. This email outlined how Carrie wanted to raise $6,000 to support six different organizations across the globe. Her desire was to give $1,000 to each organization and she shared what the impact of each of those investments would be.

Carrie reached into her contact list and sent the email to all of her friends and family. Within a couple of weeks, she had raised $6,054. She was very proud of her efforts and was excited to get the money into the hands of those in need. That was, until she received an email from a gentleman whom she had met at a conference just a few weeks earlier.

The email read: *How do I donate $1,000,000 to the Global Good Fund?*

Now, Carrie was extremely suspicious and thought that this was one of her good friends who was spoofing her. Honestly, she had met this wealthy philanthropist for 15 minutes, and why would he be offering her one million dollars? She replied to the email with a snarky tone. If the emailer was serious, he should meet her the following day for lunch with a certified check for that amount, and they could discuss it.

The next hour seemed like a blur to Carrie.

When Carrie showed up at the restaurant the next day, she was shocked to see the man she had recently met. Not only was he there, but he was also holding a certified check for $1 million made out to the Global Good Fund. She was so convinced it would be one of her friends showing up and holding a phony check, the joke would be short and sweet. Boy was Carrie wrong!

The next hour seemed like a blur to Carrie. They talked about the impact that she could make with this money and what the next steps would be. As she left the luncheon, there were still so many questions to be answered. She was holding a check made out to an organization that didn't even exist! The Global Good Fund was the subject line of an email, not a nonprofit organization that could accept the funds ... at least, not yet. Additionally, she was an important executive at INOVA. What would happen to all her responsibilities? On Carrie's walk back to her office from lunch, there were so many thoughts running through her head. What was she to do?

Arriving back at INOVA, she went directly to her boss' office and threw the check on his desk. She said, "Look what a little bit of money did!"

The boss' initial gift of one hundred dollars had now turned into over $1,000,000. To her amazement, her boss said to her, "At INOVA, you work for me. At the Global Good Fund, I work for you." In addition, he said, "I am going to match the one million dollars."

Now Carrie had over $2,000,000 to go change the world. In that moment, she knew her life had changed forever. The idea for the Global Good Fund was born and Carrie went to work. She gathered many of the smartest people she knew and crafted a plan to support socially-minded business leaders and start a fellowship program for them.

Carrie Rich had a vision and built a plan to execute it. She focused on women leaders of social enterprises and nonprofits that had a chance to change the world. Over the past 13 years, the Global Good Fund has supported well over 240

Carrie has followed her passion and her purpose.

entrepreneurs, guided countless civic leaders, and has built a support system including some of the most talented mentors you could imagine.

In addition to mentoring, Carrie realized that many of these leaders would need capital in order to add fuel to their projects. The Global Good Fund had helped transform many of these concepts into thriving businesses, and who better to invest in their future than the organization that helped them prosper? In 2016, she decided to launch the first Global Impact Fund and piloted her next idea. Today, she has raised close to $10 million to invest in early-stage social impact businesses and is building the foundation for a future that is bright and powerful.

Carrie has followed her passion and her purpose. She has connected with others that have aligned values and vision and is making an incredible impact on the world. When Carrie joined INOVA straight out of Georgetown University, I don't believe she ever envisioned herself on the path she is currently on. In her mind, she would have been the CEO of a growing capitalistic business that would be driving our economy.

That didn't happen. What happened is far more important. She is still extremely focused on achievement, but her definition of success is extremely different from what it was a decade ago.

Carrie is just one example of redirecting capital but not financial capital … intellectual capital. Why can't we look at Carrie as an example of what a generous investment can do to transform a life and have that life transform a portion of our society?

- What if we could scale this idea?

- What if we invested in young people to help them use their brilliance to effect social change rather than putting them on the hamster wheel of life to accumulate wealth?

- What if this was the path we created so that at some point in the future they could use the result of their work and their wealth creation to make an impact?

The time has come for us to reimagine what social change can look like, to reimagine how we use and put our human capital to work in our society. The time has come to say that we have enough, and we need to create more resources for change, using people's skills to improve the world around us, not just our world. What we need is more joy. We need to be redirecting capital, human capital, to focus on projects of impact, not just projects that produce financial return!

Carrie Rich has been one of my greatest teachers. She walks through every situation with grace and simplicity. When things come up, she doesn't react and get emotional. She responds thoughtfully about how she can make the best out of every situation. She is amazing, yet the biggest lesson she has taught me is that I need to be doing work that feeds my soul, that makes a difference in the world.

Lessons I Learned from Carrie …

For 20 years I built a business and used the proceeds from that business to make an impact. For most of the people I've met on my journey, that is enough for them. They can deal with clients they don't love and provide them great service while making an impact on the side. That is not my truth, and now I know why. What works for me doesn't need to work for anyone else in the world. This is about what feeds my soul.

I am here to attract those who see the world the way that I do. I have an amazing aptitude for connecting great human beings to each other. Many have told me that my skill set is extremely unique, and it has served me very well in my life. That is my truth, and that is what I need to do to fill my cup and make the impact I know I'm here to make.

Thank you, Carrie Rich, for knowing what you are, who you are, and why you are here!

5

The Identity Illusion

The world of being a competitive Paralympic triathlete was starting to paint a picture.

Over my lifetime, I have met some remarkable people that have faced more adversity than most. In recent years I've gotten heavily involved with an organization in San Diego called the Challenged Athletes Foundation (CAF). CAF has introduced me to hundreds of individuals who are living amazing lives, even though many would call them challenged, even damaged.

My journey with CAF started on a bike ride during COVID in 2021. I was riding on the 101 in Carlsbad, California, and stopped at a traffic light next to another biker, a slightly built man wearing a CAF jersey—Jonathan Collopy. I spoke with him about joining a bike club, and he suggested that I join CAF's club. He said the club was meeting up again in April, and I should meet him any Saturday at 8 a.m. behind the Flower Hill Mall in Del Mar, a town north of San Diego.

I showed up for my first ride with CAF members and met some amazing people. There were athletes of all shapes and sizes, including a good friend, Eric Northbrook, who had broken his back in a motorcycle accident in 2006. There were plenty of able-bodied riders as well, most of them were talking about training for a program commonly referred to as "MDC." Eric was riding a recumbent hand cycle that is beyond epic. Eric had mentioned something called MDC before, yet I never understood what he was talking about. I learned quickly.

That first morning, I also ran into a woman named Carol Corcoran, who heard my shoes on the gravel and she said hello to me. I looked at her and responded, "Hello," yet she didn't look back at me. What I saw were big, dark goggles. Carol is blind and was riding on the back of a tandem bike. Her captain was Tom, and I told them to enjoy the ride and thought nothing of the encounter.

On my first ride up the coast, from Del Mar to Oceanside and back, I had conversations with so many people. About halfway through the ride, Tom and Carol sped by me, and I thought to myself, I could see myself on the front of a tandem one day. That looked fun. Little did I know how fortuitous that thought was.

About two months later, I saw Carol again. This time she was preparing to get on a different bicycle with a different captain—Sargent Major Brian Milton. Brian and I started talking, and I asked him how Carol found different captains to ride with her. Brian told me about the Blind Stoker Club (BSC) and gave me the website information. That afternoon I submitted a form on the website, and the wheels were in motion.

Meet Jeff Mata

Over the next month I was given a tandem bike by the BSC and was provided with training from Susan Stewart, who trains all the captains for BSC. The next few weeks were so much fun. I learned to control a tandem, how to start and stop and how to care for my Stoker when one rode with me. Susan reminded me that these individuals were putting their lives in my hands so it was a big responsibility.

Remember that thing called the MDC? Well, the MDC is the Million Dollar Challenge. It's a ride from San Francisco to San Diego that CAF coordinates each October and is magical. I had decided when I joined the club that I was going to participate in the MDC that year or the following year. So, now that I was training to be a captain of a tandem, what would be better than doing that ride with one of the CAF athletes? I told the founder of the BSC that if he gave me a blind athlete as my Stoker, I would do the MDC with him or her. That's when I was introduced to Jeff Mata. Let me tell you Jeff's story.

Blind Ambition

It was a cool Saturday in April of 2022, and after six hours, 53 minutes and 53 seconds, Jeff stood at the finish line of his first half Ironman with his partner, Sargent Major Brian Milton. Jeff had learned to swim only six months earlier when he decided to participate in the CAF mini triathlon in October.

Jeff is beyond motivated. He is an international Jiu-Jitsu champion, owns his own Jiu-Jitsu gym in Poway, California, and lives most of the time on his own. What sets Jeff apart from anyone else I've met in my life is his understanding of what's important in life. Jeff has a deep desire to compete and to win, yet if he doesn't win, he gives himself 24 hours to complain about it, then it's off to the next challenge.

Jeff Mata was born to a Philippine family that emigrated to the US. He was one of two sons and lived a very active life through his early 20s. Jeff loved sports, motorcycles, wrestling, and boxing. And he loved to push the boundaries. He and his brother caused a bit of trouble growing up. Jeff was the younger of the two, a bit shy, and on the smaller side.

In high school he decided to focus on wrestling as his main sport and his life started to change. Jeff became more confident, was becoming an excellent athlete, and by his senior year in high school, he was the #8 ranked wrestler in his weight class in California. He loved his coach; he loved his team. And life seemed to be going so well, until it all ended when he lost his #1 position on his team to a younger wrestler.

This was supposed to be his year, the one where he competed in state competitions and got all the accolades. It didn't turn out that way, and Jeff decided to quit the team. His coach was extremely disappointed, but Jeff was adamant that he could do this on his own. This was becoming a theme for him … needing to do things on his own.

At the age of 26, Jeff was competing as an amateur boxer in San Diego. As is his nature, he was extremely competitive. During a specific match in 2008, he was struck in the head numerous times by his opponent. A few days later he started to develop blurry vision and went to see an eye doctor. The doctor examined Jeff's left eye and informed him that he had a detached retina and that he would need surgery within 48 hours or he would likely go blind. This doctor was young and passionate, and told Jeff one way to proceed in his situation. However, the surgery he suggested was extremely risky and could cause challenges in the future.

Jeff found another specialist, an older and wiser eye specialist, who told Jeff that if he did the surgery, it wouldn't work, and he would risk the opportunity to repair his eyes in the future. Jeff and his family were confused, so he found a third opinion from one of the top eye doctors in Southern California. This third doctor agreed with the seasoned specialist and recommended that Jeff not have any surgery at that time.

Over the coming weeks, Jeff lost total sight in both eyes and today, is totally blind. There was nothing that they could do to save his sight based on the available technology.

The next year was a blur, literally and figuratively. He turned to partying and numbing the pain

Jeff, in his mind, had lost everything.

of what had happened. He spiraled into a hole that seemed to keep getting deeper. He found comfort in cocaine and alcohol and for a year he drowned himself in these vices. This numbing turned to ideas of suicide, and one long, dark day in 2009, he took an entire bottle of pills to end it all.

When Jeff was boxing, he was in the welterweight class at 155 pounds. One year after losing his sight, this 5' 8" man now weighed in at over 220 pounds. Jeff, in his mind, had lost everything.

Happily, Jeff's suicide attempt failed, yet his journey had just begun. Over the next few years, he continued to battle with depression and needed to find a way out. He needed to find a passion for life again and to reconnect with those who loved him. His parents are amazing people, yet they had never experienced blindness in their family before, so they had no idea how to support him. Ultimately, it was up to Jeff to decide how his story would play out.

It took about five years for Jeff to accept the fact that he was blind. And when he did, his life changed forever. Over the past decade, he has graduated from college, become a world champion in Brazilian Jiu-Jitsu, and launched multiple businesses. His life is full and focuses on his physical health and wellness as he prepares to become a triathlete. The world of becoming a competitive Paralympic triathlete was starting to paint a future for Jeff that was filled with purpose, meaning, and challenge.

When I met Jeff in September of 2021, through the Blind Stokers Club (BSC), he was still wondering what to focus on in his life. He had won some international Jiu-Jitsu competitions and was involved in the US Judo team. He had started to get involved with tandem cycling and was participating with the BSC. The BSC is a collection of sighted and blind individuals who love to cycle. The group is focused on tandem bicycle riding. The front person on a tandem is called the captain, and the person in the back is called the Stoker. Hence the name of the organization, Blind Stokers. Over the past few years, I have had the privilege of spending many hours on a bicycle with Jeff and not only hearing his story but getting to be part of his world.

Jeff shares openly about his challenges and his visions for the future. He is happy, has a lot of wonderful people in his life, and is more deeply connected in every part of his life than he ever was when he was sighted.

I mentioned earlier about the MDC ride with CAF. In 2022, Jeff and I had the privilege to join 160 other cyclists on the 640 mile ride from San Francisco to San Diego. We spent over a year training before doing the ride and had an amazing experience together. It all started at the San Diego Airport on October 14, as we waited to board our flight. Since Jeff is blind, the gate attendant gave us special treatment. After being checked in for the flight, we went off to hang as a group with the Sargent Major.

About 30 minutes later we wondered when we were going to board. Returning to the ticket counter, it turned out that our flight had already taken off without us. We had missed hearing all of the boarding call announcements. The gate agent was in a bit of a bind since we were on the manifest for the previous flight. It all worked out in the end. We boarded the next flight and found our bags waiting for us, having arrived on the previous flight. The good news was that CAF had shipped our bikes to San Francisco earlier in the week. When Jeff and I finally arrived at the airport, we picked up our bags and headed to the hotel.

The next seven days were some of the most magical and physically challenging days of my life. On October 15 we stood outside the hotel, dressed in our bike gear with 160 other cyclists, including three other tandems, and started the ride. Day one was from San Francisco to Santa Cruz. That day was exhilarating with the last 25 miles of the 85-mile ride and 4,500 feet of climb in a slightly cold mist. That did not feel great, yet it was all part of our journey.

When we got to our first hotel, there were lines for the masseurs—several of them. This was a first for me and a pleasant surprise. I found out there would be masseurs at every stop along the ride. After a quick massage, the hot tub welcomed my tired body and then we went to dinner. After dinner on the first night, I was told that Jeff was going to be on a panel with the other blind riders to speak with the entire group. Little did I know that they wanted the captains on the panel as well.

For the next hour, the four tandem pairs had the opportunity to share their stories. One of the captains had lost her leg in a bike accident. So, her tandem had two challenged athletes on it! It was a magical evening that I will never forget.

Day two was a blur as we rode from Santa Cruz to Big Sur. The ride was around 87 miles with 4,500 feet of climb through Carmel, past all the multimillion dollar homes and the famous golf courses, Pebble Beach and Cypress Hill. When we got to the lodge in Big Sur, we all knew that the next day was the big day: 118 miles and 7,500 feet of climb. We started Day three with a multi-mile climb up the mountain. I was so pumped and excited for the day. We got to the top of the mountain and started to speed down the back side. One turn after the next provided views that were magical. At each turn, I would say, "Holy Shit" to Jeff, and he would say, "What's wrong?"

That was one of the most exhilarating days of my life!

I said, "I can't believe that this view is more beautiful than the last turn!" How do you describe what I was seeing to a blind person? Then I remembered that Jeff was fully sighted before he was blind. I described the beauty of the ocean colors, and how high the crisp blue water hit the rocks, along with the shades of the colors of the plants and everything else. Later, he told me that my narration was amazing and brought it all alive for him. For the next eight hours, we pedaled, we sweated, we passed riders, riders passed us, and we continued the climb.

Before the last big climb into Pismo Beach, our stop for the night, there was the famous bridge on the 101. All the bikers gathered at a rest area about 500 yards before the bridge. The video crew had a drone that they were using to collect aerial footage and they wanted everyone to cross the bridge at the same time. Our ride leader, one of my angels, Renee Milton, had Jeff and me lead the whole pack across the bridge. We attacked the next few hills and then made the final descent into Pismo Beach. That was one of the most exhilarating days of my life!

We all slept well that night. It had been an amazing day. But the next day's ride was the one I was most worried about. I had never done more than 90 miles in a day before the MDC, and now I had been doing back-to-back centuries. Day four was 114 miles with 4,700 feet of climb. When we got on the bike that morning, I told Jeff that this was his day. If I was by myself, I'm not sure I would have gotten on the bike that morning. I was exhausted!

Day five was another long eight-plus-hour day. I was grateful when we wheeled into Santa Barbara. That day taught me a lot about myself and what I was capable of. Jeff and I spent a lot of time together on that bike, and the conversations were something I will never forget. The only slowdown was the two flat tires, both on the same day, and nothing else happened the rest of the trip. From Santa Barbara, we headed to Long Beach, and from Long Beach, we headed to Dana Point for the end of day six.

The last evening at Dana Point included a gala where we raised over $1.8 million dollars. The event was magical and the camaraderie was off the charts. I hadn't felt that close to so many awesome people in my life. Besides the four tandems with blind athletes, there were champion hand cyclists, dozens of athletes with prosthetic legs, and some in recumbent bikes. The community that CAF has built is pure magic and the love that was in the room that night will be felt in my heart for the rest of my life.

Day seven was the shortest ride of all, 56 miles and about 2,000 feet of climb from Dana Point to La Jolla Shores. I never could have imagined completing that ride, and there I was with Jeff at the finish line as my family showed up to support us. My son was so excited to hang the medal for finishing the ride around my neck. Of all the accomplishments I have had in my life, the MDC ride with Jeff is at the top of the list.

Jeff and I have spoken about the chance that he might get his sight back. Doctors have told him that if surgical procedures improve, his blindness might be reversible. If Jeff were given the opportunity to see again, he's not sure if he would take advantage of it. He has learned to live in the world differently. His sense of smell, hearing, and energy is off the charts.

His ability to compete in Jiu-Jitsu competitions with sighted individuals is amazing; and his ability to feel body movement is enhanced by his blindness.

Jeff can sense a person's movement before they even move. When we ride on a tandem, he can sense when there is a challenge and has reacted even faster than a sighted person might on a bike. His ability to smell and sense odors from far away has provided him an advantage over the rest of us. When they are pleasant, the aromas are a gift.

Most importantly, beyond all the sensory advantages his blindness has created, Jeff is so connected to others as a person. He is so present. When you are with him, you feel like the only person in the world. Jeff can connect with people in an instant. He also has a sense of calm and presence that he never had as a sighted person. In his own words, "My life is so much richer now than it ever was when I could see."

Jeff Mata is an amazing person who happens to be blind. His blindness has caused hardship and pain, yet that pain has produced a world he loves, and there are so many who truly love him as well. In the end, as is true of each of the people profiled in this book, the power of human connection is what guides Jeff's life. His desire to be engaged with others and connect on a deeper, more meaningful level might never have happened had he not lost his sight.

I applaud him for his perseverance and his ability to find the good in what life has delivered to his doorstep.

Lessons I Learned from Jeff ...

Jeff has taught me a great deal on my journey. He has been an example of strength during the hardest times. He possesses patience and determination that are truly uncommon. Jeff is an amazing athlete. Watching him maneuver effortlessly through his day is absolutely awe-inspiring. Our seven days together riding down the coast of California will be etched in my mind forever.

Thank you, Jeff Mata, for knowing what you are, who you are, and why you are here.

A Warrior's Aim

And then, a voice surfaced: "You are mine. You are mine."

As I was preparing to write this section of the book, I spoke with Nico Marcolongo at CAF. Nico is one of the main liaisons between the organization and the athletes. He has been with CAF for 17 years and is a veteran. I asked him to help me find an athlete who walked the planet with joy and had an amazing backstory. He mentioned a few names and sent out an email to those he thought would be a good fit for this book. I received an email from Samantha Moon Tucker saying that she would be open to an interview.

I went on *YouTube* and watched an interview with Bob Babbit, one of the cofounders of CAF, and Moon. Moon's light and energy were infectious, and I knew that her story must be included in *The Joy Molecule*. At this point in my journey, it is always a pleasure to meet those who walk this planet in light and know what they are, who they are, and why they are here.

Meet Moon Tucker

Moon Tucker has lived many lives. She was born in a small town, raised under the watchful eye of a strong but unaffectionate grandfather. He had wanted a boy, so he called her Sam. Her mother named her Melissa. Her father called her Moonwalker. That early confusion over her identity lingered for years, shaping a life of emotional dissonance.

Her grandfather treated her like the grandson he never had, putting her to work daily on the ranch. Moon internalized the message: love was conditional, performance was mandatory, and nowhere was safe. When her mom remarried and moved them away at age six, it wasn't an escape. It was simply a new setting for the same emotional script.

She spent her younger years chasing and giving the familiar coldness she'd grown up with—relationships that mirrored her grandfather's detachment, resulting in multiple divorces, estranged children, and a self-described train wreck of a life. As a child, she learned a local man had died by suicide, and the seed of that idea took root. It was her daily focus for decades.

Motherhood came early. The Air Force offered structure, purpose, and escape. She found a path forward in public affairs and began again in Italy, toddler in tow. But despite the fresh start, she hadn't rewritten the story of her identity or worth.

By 41, Moon had divorced a third time. Her kids no longer spoke to her. She had hit bottom. With death her focus, she asked a friend to help her get deployed to Afghanistan. *If I am going to die, it might as well be in service—more honorable than suicide,* she thought.

On October 8, 2010, Moon got on her Harley after a long, grueling day. She was emotionally wrecked, crying as she rode a lonely stretch of highway outside of Ft. Knox. That's when she hit a patch of crushed asphalt. The bike spun out, the throttle stuck, and her sleeve got sucked into the drive belt. The Harley dragged her by her arm down the highway. A foot pedal she'd installed—just days before—kept the bike from crushing her completely. Her left arm was pulled into the screaming wheel, shredding it to the bone. She was being burned alive.

Then: silence. Moon felt like she was floating through space. No sound. No pain. Just sparks trailing behind her in the dark. Her legs bounced on the pavement behind the bike, and yet, she couldn't feel anything.

And then came the breath.

The first deep breath she'd ever consciously taken. Then a second. She savored it, not knowing if it would be her last. In that moment, she surrendered. Gratitude filled her. Time stopped. Her mind went quiet.

And then, a voice surfaced: "You are mine. You are mine."

At once, she saw her entire life. It was like looking at the lights of cities on earth from the heavens, representing her choices, beliefs, and lies she had mistaken for truth. In an instant, her identity collapsed. Like a table with broken legs, her old belief system fell away. For the first time, Moon Tucker felt truly alive.

She didn't care if she lived or died. In that moment, there was no fear, no judgment—just oneness. She belonged to everything, and everything belonged to her.

In the hospital, doctors gave her a choice: attempt to save her mangled arm or amputate. It had been ground to the bone, nothing remained but trauma. She chose amputation. After many surgeries, she now lives with an arm constructed from her abdominal tissue.

When she left the hospital, the rest of her life fell apart—but it didn't matter. TNone of it mattered anymore. Now, she was free.

She moved to Idaho to stay with family she hadn't seen in years. She began running, kayaking—following her intuition for the first time. That same intuition led her to California, where she met Jeff Fabry, a Paralympic archer. He saw her shoot once and said, "You're a natural. No bad habits. If you listen to everything I say, I think you can make the Paralympic team in 19 months."

She did.

Moon moved to Colorado Springs to train, despite the Olympic Training Center not having an archery facility. She found one elsewhere. Six months later, she made Team USA. Two months after that, she made the world team.

Archery wasn't just a sport; it was her transformation.

Through the discipline of the bow, Moon discovered her body. She learned how the nervous system works, how the subconscious runs our lives, and how old programming can be rewritten. It felt like someone had handed her a user manual for being human.

She just didn't survive. She *transformed*.

But she never forgot the ditch.

How do you go from suicide to joyfulness in 30 seconds? That question launched her next chapter. Moon immersed herself in neurology, neuro-linguistic programming (NLP), and Spiral Somatics. She studied the body-mind-spirit connection to understand the animation of her soul.

In 2016—six years after lying shattered on the roadside— Moon Tucker stood tall on the world stage in Rio de Janeiro.

She was the first woman to represent Team USA in Paralympic compound archery.

She just didn't survive. She *transformed*.

Today, Moon mentors new amputees. She works with a nonprofit that supports individuals with physical and cognitive disabilities. Audiences are enthralled when she speaks at schools and veteran events. She advocates for inclusive sports and inner understanding.

Her story resonates not because she overcame, but because she transcended. She doesn't present herself as a hero. She shows up as a mirror, inviting others to see themselves in her journey.

Her *What* has evolved: from soldier to athlete to guide. Her *Who* is steady, grounded, and fiercely compassionate. Her *Why* is luminous: to remind us that joy is always present in wreckage.

Moon doesn't preach hope; she *embodies* it.

When you sit with her today, her smile lights up the room. Her energy is calm, yet radiant. There's peace in her that draws you in.

Her life hasn't changed; it's come full circle.

Lessons I Learned from Moon ...

When I spoke with Moon, her presence was her greatest lesson. She was present. She was joyful. And she was filled with life. Moon spoke about her ego and her identity and how those had shaped her decisions in life, yet they were not true. I learned from her sharing that her story was not the truth. It was only her story, and that her training in life from an early age had formed who she thought she was. It was that moment of being dragged down the highway and losing her arm that taught her who she was, which makes me question so many beliefs I have had in my life.

Thank you, Moon Tucker, for knowing What you are, Who you are, and Why you are here!

Losing Identity, Again

Life's setbacks can strip away the layers we once thought defined us ... they also offer the chance to discover a deeper, more authentic self.

In 2021, an app was blowing up online called Clubhouse. It was a unique chat room where online users could show up with their voice to get to know others who cared about the same things you did. Sessions would take place at specific times, and you could get to know people from around the world.

One morning, I was in a room on Clubhouse and spoke with a bunch of people about purpose and meaning. On the call was a man named Joe. When we were introducing ourselves, I mentioned that I rode bikes with CAF and he said he was a CAF athlete. We decided to share our contact information and follow up at some point in the future. A few weeks later, we connected on a Zoom call and started talking. And Joe shared his story.

Growing up, Joe played any and every sport possible. He was a promising college football player but that opportunity ended at age 19 when he was in a boating accident. His neck was broken. Joe is a paraplegic who is uber competitive, and following his accident, he found the sport of wheelchair rugby. In our conversation, he mentioned not making the Paralympic team in 2016 and that his identity had been ripped from him for the second time.

As we were getting to know each other, I asked him how he paid for his living expenses. He said that playing wheelchair rugby for the US National team paid some money, and he also mentioned that he was a public speaker. Now, that is something that I know about. I love public speaking and have been on many stages in my life. I never met a microphone that I didn't like.

When I asked Joe what his keynote topic was, I knew he was going to tell me *Overcoming Adversity,* because that is what every CAF athlete talks about. I said to Joe, "Can you please do me a favor?"

He said, "Sure, what is it?" I told him that as an able-bodied person, I can't identify with the topic of overcoming adversity from someone in a wheelchair. He has gone through something that I can identify with. He said, "What do you mean?"

I said, "At your next speech, can you please talk about losing identity? That is a topic that everyone can relate to." When I told him that, he was quiet for a moment. Over the next few months, we spoke regularly about his speaking, and now Joe speaks about "identity" and his purpose, and how it has affected his life.

Meet Joe Delegrave

It was July 19, 2016. Joe Delegrave sat in the coach's office. He had just finished a grueling week of tryouts to make the 2016 Paralympics for the US Wheelchair Rugby Team. The first three days of the tryouts were brutal. For three solid days, the only thing they did was eat, then practice, eat, then practice, eat, then practice, and then go to sleep. They did that for three straight days. Joe was in the best shape of his life, doing everything he thought he needed to do to make the team.

Joe had been the co-captain of the team for several years, and he was excited to participate in the games in Rio to avenge a loss at the 2012 Olympics in London during the Gold Medal Game to Team Canada. It was a long four years, including some amazing wins around the globe in 2014 and 2015. There were so many twists and turns between 2012 and 2016, yet Joe did not see what was coming. After the loss in 2012, Joe was so focused on winning and avenging that gold medal game loss that he put everything else in his life on pause. He was singularly focused on the team, and his identity was completely tied to winning gold in 2016.

It turns out that Joe had some history with the new team coach who had been his co-captain from previous years. **Another moment had irrevocably altered Joe's course.** Much of their history was not positive. This new coach had something else in mind … he wanted to make life hell for Joe, and he succeeded. Joe did not make the team. He was named an alternate, which was even worse than not being selected. As an alternate, he was required to attend all the trainings yet wasn't invited to join the team in Rio.

Joe Delegrave is a remarkable human being. At 19 years old, standing 6 feet, 6 inches tall and weighing 260 pounds, he played tight end at Winona State University. After his freshman year, he came home for the summer of 2004, and on July 10 his life changed forever.

Long before the rejection for the 2016 Paralympics, another moment had irrevocably altered Joe's course. It was a bright July day in 2004, and Joe was enjoying a carefree afternoon on a 14 foot bass-fishing boat with his best friends, Kyle and Adam. The river was calm, the back slue gentle—a perfect setting for youth and camaraderie. Joe sat comfortably in his familiar fishing chair, a small pole in hand, immersed in the simple joys of the water.

Then, without warning, the routine shattered. The bottom of the boat caught on a hidden obstacle beneath the river's surface, and in a heartbeat, the boat lurched to a stop. Joe was violently hurled backward; his head collided with the interior of the boat, and in that brutal instant, time seemed to slow. When he came to, the reassuring presence of his friends was replaced by a dawning horror.

Their voices filled the air with anxious questions, but as Joe reached down, he discovered that the familiar sensation of his legs was gone, numb and unresponsive. In that single, devastating moment, Joe Delegrave became a quadriplegic. His neck was broken.

The accident robbed him not only of his mobility but of the physical identity he had so long embraced. No longer could he lean on his athletic prowess as the core of who he was. Instead, the wreckage of that day forced him to embark on a deeper journey, a quest to understand himself beyond the physical realm.

Compounding these physical and emotional upheavals was a lifelong struggle with a fractured relationship with his father. Joe's father was a man marked by absence and inconsistency, often in and out of prison from the time Joe was a young child until he was an adult. The few memories that remained were bittersweet: the giant, lovingly made birthday cookie from behind prison walls; the rare hugs that hinted at love; and the letters filled with promises of pride and hope. Yet, these fleeting moments were shadowed by years of abandonment and unresolved longing.

When Joe finally met his father again in a stark visitation room, he saw not only the man who had failed him but also a reflection of what might have been. In that raw encounter, Joe found the strength to forgive—a necessary step to reclaim the parts of himself that had been lost in bitterness. This act of forgiveness became a cornerstone of his transformation, teaching him that healing often begins with letting go of the past.

Today, Joe Delegrave stands as a testament to the power of inner transformation. No longer defined solely by the medals he once pursued or by the role he played on the wheelchair rugby team, Joe has forged a new identity rooted in the core principles encapsulated by the acronym SELF: Strengths, Emotions, Leadership, and Focus. These values guide his every action, reflecting a belief in a higher purpose that transcends the physical limitations he now lives with.

Joe's journey—from the shattering impact of that fateful boat accident, to the crushing disappointment of Olympic rejection, and through the painful healing of a fractured paternal bond, Joe's truth has been revealed that resonates deeply within him. True identity is not measured by physical prowess or external accolades. It is nurtured in the crucible of adversity and reborn through forgiveness, connection, and an unwavering commitment to core values.

In redefining himself, Joe Delegrave has emerged not as the athlete he once was but as a man of profound resilience

Strengths, Emotions, Leadership, and Focus guide his every action.

and purpose. His story is a powerful reminder that while life's setbacks can strip away the layers you once thought defined you, they also offer the chance to discover a deeper, more authentic self. One that stands tall on the foundations of Strength, Emotions, Leadership, and Focus.

Joe retired from competition after the Tokyo 2020 Paralympic Games, where the USA wheelchair rugby team took the silver. He was named interim head coach of the US team, then coach for the Paraplegic Wheelchair Rugby team. And he will be the coach of the Paraplegic Olympics in 2028.

Lessons I Learned from Joe ...

Joe Delegrave has been one of my best teachers for understanding how much my identity and my ego have gotten in my way. I have had the pleasure of helping him on his journey and seeing his spirit regularly, even with challenges in front of him. He is a blessing. Joe has lost his identity multiple times, once on the river and a second time in 2016, but these identities did not keep him from accessing his true self.

I am proud to call Joe Delegrave a good friend and know that his strength is rooted deeply inside of him.

Thank you, Joe, for knowing what you are, who you are, and why you are here.

6

Persistence, Perseverance, and Patience

She walks this earth every day knowing that she is capable and that she makes a difference.

It was early 2011 and I had recently moved to San Diego. I had just published the first version of my second book, *Break Points*. It was a labor of love project that I enjoyed immensely. I was very proud of the book and had sold about 1,000 copies to some of the major manufacturers in the IT Channel. Cisco was a big partner at the time, as was Catalyst Telecom, Avnet and a few others that bought the books in bulk to give to their reseller partners.

I was on an escalator in LA at a book event and locked eyes with a woman going down the escalator as I was going up. There are some people you see in your life that you were just meant to meet. Judith Briles is one of those people for me. It turns out that she was a speaker at the event and had a booth. I found her later that morning. At that time Judith had written dozens of books and was positioned in the market as The Book Shepherd, coaching and guiding others to successful publishing. As of the publication of this book, she has personally written 48 books and has worked with over 1,000 authors in guiding them to publication. I showed her my book and she said that the book deserved better.

The cover of the book was black with a broken chain across the front. I had the cover designed by my marketing agency, not a book design firm, and Judith could tell. She told me that you don't design book covers in black for the leadership genre. That's a no-no! For the next year, we worked together to republish *Break Points,* and the second version is much better than the original. I have often heard that the best books are not written, rather they are rewritten. And Judith showed me how.

I stayed in touch with her over the years, and we've become great friends. Judith helped me indie-publish *Success Redefined* in 2015, and now she is helping me bring *The Joy Molecule* to market. I would not have included Judith in this book if she didn't walk the planet knowing what she is, who she is, and why she is here.

Meet Judith Briles

Judith lives an amazingly full life, filled with ups and lots of downs. She has traveled around the sun 79 times. She has seen so much good, experienced so much pain, shared her story with thousands of audiences, and affected many, many lives, including mine.

On September 3, 1983, her life changed forever. On that day, the unthinkable happened: her 19-year-old son fell off an abandoned bridge, the Dumbarton Bridge near Palo Alto, California.

From a young age, Judith was aware that she was smart. She could run circles around most everyone around her. She was observant of the world and her role in it. She found comfort in her childhood caretakers, friends, and those who demonstrated what she understood love to be. She didn't receive love from her parents or her three brothers. She only felt pain and abandonment. On that day in 1983, no matter what had happened in the past, nor what might happen in the future, her life was forever changed.

During her childhood, Judith realized that her parents were not very good or kind people. She didn't complain about it; she found solutions. Whether it was finding comfort with the family caregiver or her best friend and their family, Judith knew that there was something better than what she was born into. She always knew that she would find her way, and no matter what was happening, she would persevere. She has also been able to do it with strength and candor. She doesn't mind sharing how strict she was with her children, or how direct she is with her adult children who now have families of their own.

Judith had felt a similar pain in her life before that day in 1983. As a child she had experienced abuse from her brothers. She had been traumatized often by her mother and others in her life. On February 15, 1971, Judith lost her fourth child, Billy, a week after he was born. After Billy's death, Judith ended her 11-year marriage and faced challenges around child custody that would never happen in today's legal system.

Never quit! Keep moving forward.

When she was getting divorced from her first husband, she was fired from her job working at a brokerage firm. She was left with nothing. Her soon-to-be ex-husband came from a wealthy family with yachts and regular weekend trips to Catalina Island. All of that came to an end when the marriage ended, and all that wealth was used to make her life miserable, including her ex bribing her lawyer to sabotage her, and he gave money to people to testify against her.

A few weeks after losing her job, a few clients she worked with asked her to go to lunch with them. At that lunch, the group handed her an envelope with $2,000 cash plus a list of firms in the financial area that they had made appointments for—even setting up interviews in four cities. They told her how talented she was, and that she was the smartest person in the office where she had been working. As one said, and the others nodded their heads in agreement, "You should be a stockbroker, not the assistant! It is time to go out and do it on your own." And that is what she did.

It was now the late 1970s, and Judith Briles was on top of the world. She had met a wonderful man, John, who she eventually married. She was a top-producing broker for EF Hutton before launching her firm—a firm that was on the appointment list she first had. Judith published her first book in 1981, titled *The Woman's Guide to Financial Savvy*. She was getting speaking opportunities across the country, and she returned to the same courtroom where she had lost everything. This time, it was the same judge who said out loud, "How did this happen to you?" She immediately received full custody of her kids. It was the only thing she had wanted. Assets were gone, and child support never came. It didn't matter. Life was moving forward, and Judith was thriving. And her kids were okay until Labor Day Weekend of 1983.

According to my research, the Dumbarton Bridge was built in 1927, and by the early 1980s CALTRANS, via the state of California, had decided to build a new bridge that would span San Francisco Bay via Route 84. The bridge had become one of the most congested commuter crossings in the Bay Area. It was only two lanes—one each way—which was insufficient for the growing volume of cars between Silicon Valley and the East Bay. Backup traffic on approach roads and safety concerns prompted urgent expansion plans. The new bridge, a 6-lane expanse, was completed in October of 1982 and improved capacity, safety, and earthquake resilience.

Even though Frank died a year after the new bridge was built, Judith shared that the city had no plans to take down the old bridge. There were numerous young people on the bridge the night Frank fell, many of them his friends. The entire community was rocked, not just Judith. Finding Frank's body took three months and was found by a fisherman. When speaking with Judith about the incident, you can feel the pain that she lived through during that time.

Judith talks about Frank with such love and joy. She remembers how talented he was, how he could fix just about anything with a wrench and a screwdriver. Frank was not meant for college. He wanted to be a mechanic, but it was not meant to be. After Frank fell from the bridge, Judith made it her mission to get that abandoned bridge torn down. She did not want another family to have to deal with the pain that she and her family had to endure.

Judith visited the area where Frank died and realized how easy it would be for anyone to get access to the old bridge. The fence protecting the abandoned bridge was laying on the ground; there was debris everywhere. In her words, "You could tell that lots of people were spending time there and no one cared. It was then that I had the words and power to take the bridge down so another child could not be harmed." So, Judith brought a lawsuit against the state of California. And she did countless interviews with the media to keep the pressure on the state.

Within three months of filing her suit, she got a call from someone who was familiar with what had happened. "It is because of you that the legislature has allocated close to $5 million to demolish the bridge." It took another year for the implosion to happen on a Sunday morning. The next day, she called her lawyers to settle their fees and to shut the suit down. She wanted no moneys. She picked up her life and moved to Colorado, where she and John live today.

Around the same time that Frank died, Judith found out that her business partner had embezzled over $1,000,000 from her, and she went broke, again. Her business partner had taken on a partner Judith knew nothing about ... cocaine.

Judith Briles walks on this earth every day knowing that she is capable and that she makes a difference. Judith shares, "No matter what is going on in your life, there are always yeses out there if you just look for them." In every situation in life, Judith sees the possibility of what might happen. She walks with pride knowing that she will always come out the other side a better person. Every day Judith practices persistence, perseverance, and patience in her life and her business.

Lessons I Learned from Judith ...

Never quit! Keep moving forward despite everything else that's going on in your life. She taught me not only to focus on my strengths, but to surround myself with others who can complete tasks so much better than I can. Judith has assembled some of the most humble and capable people to work on her projects. She is masterful at that, and I thank her for all the amazing work she has done for me over the past 15 years. She is the poster child for persistence, perseverance, and patience.

Thank you, Judith, for knowing what you are, who you are, and why you are here.

7

The Enough Academy

I like looking someone in the eye and knowing his or her life is going to change. That's where the joy comes from.

It was 2016 and I was speaking with Miles Rose, an old friend from New York. Miles was telling me about someone he thought I should know when I shared about my travels around the globe and my desire to create impact. "Larry … you need to meet my friend Irving," came across my cell phone. "Irving had sold a bank for a lot of money and is making a real impact in the world with what he is doing now."

I reached out to Irving, and it turns out that we had a major project in common. Irving was the Chairman of the Board of Digital Divide Data. DDD was part of my story with Armstrong, who you met in Chapter 3, *Circumstance Does Not Define You*. I shared that the COO of DDD spent time with Armstrong in Nairobi in 2013. This individual was helping me decide if I was making a sound investment in this ambitious young man's future or wasting my time.

Irving and his wife Stephanie have been extremely blessed in their life, and they know that those blessings do not define them. They know that the money that they possess is just energy and it is theirs to steward in the community.

Meet Irving Levin

Irving Levin didn't set out to be a philanthropist. He didn't even want to go to college. Growing up in a modest Indiana town near Chicago, he was the third of four children. The family lived in the same house until Irving left after high school. But traditional paths didn't interest him. He was a lousy student and school bored him. The structure of it felt too confining.

Music, though—music made sense to him.

Irving discovered the cello early and quickly developed real talent. After graduating from high school with no plans, he hit the road and hitchhiked around and then came home. It was then that he got the spark to take music seriously. He shared, "I was told I had talent when I was young but didn't work to develop it … at first." Eventually, he earned a scholarship to a Chicago conservatory, joined the musicians' union, and built a career playing everything from classical to rock to musical theater. That path eventually led him to Mexico, where he played in orchestras in Guadalajara and Mexico City.

By the time he was 22, Irving had lived more lives than most. But even then, he sensed he hadn't yet found his purpose.

He returned to the States and enrolled in college on a conditional basis. And in his words, he jokingly said, "A place dumb enough to take me." He studied hard, played music to pay the bills, and eventually earned an MBA. From there, his career took a new shape: a job at a record company, a pivot into finance, and eventually a move to Visa, then still a small but fast-growing company.

Over time, Irving climbed the ranks and took on larger roles, including launching the first credit card special-purpose bank

Not just any education, but the kind that lifts first-generation students into opportunity.

in the country. After a successful run, he left to replicate the business privately, and it worked. "I left Visa after four years, and moved on to consulting, and eventually to a company that asked me to start the credit card bank." In less than a decade, his company grew from a basement operation into a 1,200-person firm that sold for hundreds of millions of dollars.

Irving was 50 years old. And suddenly, he had more money than he'd ever imagined.

That moment became a dividing line. "Not that I hadn't earned it," he said, "but it still came down to a stroke of the pen. And after that, everything changed."

Irving and Stephanie immediately set aside a significant portion of their wealth to begin giving. They launched both a donor-advised fund and a private foundation—without a clear road map, just the intention to contribute. "We had no idea what we were doing," Irving shared. Then he added, "But we knew we wanted to do something meaningful."

At first, their philanthropy covered a wide spectrum: health care, social justice, international development, and environmental work. But over time, they found themselves drawn repeatedly to one area: education. Not just any education, but the kind that lifts first-generation students into opportunity. Those who were financially needy.

It started at Portland State University, where they funded a small number of scholarships for students whose families had never attended college. Many of these students were working full-time jobs, supporting their families, and attending school all at once. The Levins were floored by their grit, humility, and courage.

I like looking someone in the eye and knowing his or her life is going to change.

"These students were heroic," Irving said. "No money, no road map, and no push from home. They still showed up and did the work."

The impact was undeniable. The Levins had found their focus.

From a handful of scholarships, the program grew steadily. Now, twenty years later, they support more than 900 students annually. By next year, they'll cross the threshold of 1,000 graduates, with thousands more lives impacted—siblings, parents, relatives, entire communities. "The ripple effect is very real," Irving said. "It's not just the student. It's everyone around them."

Each scholarship is $5,000 per year and renewable throughout college—a level of long-term support that's surprisingly rare. But the money is only part of it. The Levins stay involved. They meet students, track their progress, and build relationships. It's a personal endeavor for them.

"I like retail philanthropy," Irving shared. "I like looking someone in the eye and knowing their life is going to change. That's where the joy comes from."

And it is joy—deep, fulfilling joy. Not the fleeting kind, but the kind that lasts because it is rooted in purpose.

Irving often talked about the word "should." He lives by it, sometimes to a fault. "I think anyone who's had the kind of good fortune I've had should be doing something meaningful with it," he stressed. "Not in an abstract way, but in a focused, make things better kind of way."

When asked what enough meant to him, Irving offered a grounded answer. Personally, he said, they've passed that line. "We sleep well at night. We pay our bills. We support our kids. That's enough." But when it comes to giving? There's no such thing. "We've built this amazing platform.

We can self-fund a thousand students each year for the foreseeable future, but we have the operational capacity to do more."

He hopes others will pick up the baton. The structure is in place. The model works. It could be replicated. But whether it scales or not, Irving is content. Not complacent—he's still tweaking and improving—but at peace with the path they've chosen.

That clarity comes, in part, from knowing that their giving is rooted in connection. He may call himself a contrarian and a lone wolf, but Irving has built a profoundly relational life. The scholarship students are not anonymous line items. They are people whose lives he and Stephanie have touched, and who have been touched by them in return.

"If you're not connected to anything," he stated, "you're out of luck. You've got to find something that matters. Something to give yourself to."

For Irving and Stephanie, that something is education. It's the lever they believe creates the greatest social mobility, the deepest transformation, and the most authentic joy.

When I asked Irving what he'd pass down to future generations, he didn't hesitate. "Gratitude," he said. "We live in an incredibly blessed place, and too many people forget that. Even with all the challenges in our country, the opportunity here is extraordinary. And if you've benefited from that, you owe something back."

That's what *The Enough Academy* is all about—not settling but seeing the moment you reach *enough* as a doorway. It's a shift from accumulation to contribution. It's a chance to align who you are with why you are. And it's a wonderful opportunity to connect with others doing the same.

It's a Small, Small World!

In 2013, I was deep into researching ways to help young people in Africa learn how to use computers. There were a few companies developing at that time who were training young people about computers in Uganda, Kenya, Rwanda, Tanzania, and other surrounding countries. One of those companies was called Digital Divide Data (DDD). After being introduced to Jeremy Hockstein, the CEO of DDD, we had a few conversations about the work we were looking to do in Uganda through the organization I was working with.

During my many conversations with Jeremy, I was introduced to a young man named Kirunda Kiruthi, who was the COO of DDD and lived in Nairobi, the same city where Armstrong was living. And in an amazing turn of fate, Kirunda was also a trained commercial pilot.

When you're an entrepreneur like me, you do your best to vet the investments that you are making. Here I was speaking with a trained pilot, living within miles of Armstrong, who desired to be a pilot, and with whom I was about to make a significant investment. I felt he was the perfect person to provide input about Armstrong's desire to be a pilot. I asked him, "Would you meet with Armstrong and then give me your feedback as to whether Armstrong is a good candidate to become a pilot?"

Kirunda agreed and met with Armstrong. After their meeting, he called me and said, "I believe that Armstrong would make a great pilot." With his words, I continued my path to support Armstrong's dream.

Years later, I learned that Irving Levin had provided a scholarship to Kirunda's brother, Kiruthi, as well as paid for some medical work for Kirunda. What a small world. It was such an amazing full circle moment for me!

Lessons I Learned from Irving ...

Irving, along with many other amazing philanthropists, has taught me the importance of focus in my giving. When I started to give, I looked at so many causes, yet I was always drawn to working with teen boys. That is the time in my life that was the most difficult, as was my son's. That has brought me to the Boys to Men Mentoring community. In addition, working with CAF has brought me so much joy and clarity, and I support that organization as much as possible. We all have a cause that is deep inside of us. What is that cause for you?

Thank you, Irving and Stephanie, for knowing what you are, who you are, and why you are here!

8

A Return to OC

Something told me I needed to be there, and now I know why.

In 2024, I returned to Opportunity Collaboration after a decade absence. Over that 10-year period I was 100% focused on building my world in San Diego and didn't need, nor want, to attend OC. Yes, I'll admit that I didn't want to attend in 2024, but something told me I needed to be there, and now I know why.

I named my latest company 5 Dots, as I am the Chief Connector of Dots. Yet the reason for the name is based on Steve Jobs' commencement speech at Stanford in 2005. In that speech Jobs opens by telling his story about connecting the dots. He shares stories about dropping out of college, which allowed him to drop into classes he found interesting.

One of those classes was a calligraphy class. He revealed in the speech that the reason that the Mac has all the different fonts was because of that class. If he had never dropped into that class, the Mac might not have had such beautiful ways to display text. He goes on to say that since Microsoft just copied everything from the Mac, it's possible that no computers would have beautiful typography options they have today if Jobs hadn't dropped out of college and discovered the world and imagination that calligraphy delivers.

The most important part of the speech for me was when he said the following:

> You cannot connect the dots looking forward; you can only connect the dots looking backwards. So, you have to trust that the dots will somehow connect in your future. You have to trust in something—your gut, destiny, life, karma, whatever. This approach has never let me down, and it has made all the difference in my life.

There was one main reason that I returned to OC in 2024. It was to meet Emanuel Trinity.

Meet Emanuel Trinity

As most Africans I have met, he goes by the name Trinity, his last name by American standards. Trinity is a street kid from the slums in Kampala, the largest city in Uganda. From birth, Trinity's life has been hard, harder than anything I could ever imagine. At the age of nine, he joined a gang with six other friends and saw four of them die in front of him in the first six months he was in it. He lived knowing that any day he could die as well.

Four years later, his gang leader was stoned to death. This was Trinity's opportunity to get out. He was approached by a group of missionaries from Northern Ireland while hiding behind a church. One of the missionaries asked Trinity a question that would change his life. "If you could get one thing that would keep you off the street, what would that be?"

Once he received the computer, his life changed forever.

Trinity responded, "If I had a computer, I would stay off the streets." Trinity wanted to play games that would distract him from the pain he'd experienced from an early age. Once he received the computer, his life changed forever. Trinity lived with that computer every day and started to realize that a different world had opened to him.

By the age of 19 he was one of the best computer designers in the slums of Kampala and got noticed by the Coca-Cola Company. He received a job as a graphic designer and within three months, he was able to get his family off the streets and into a safer place to live. Over the next few months, something was gnawing at him. There were still so many in the slums who were brilliant, but they were stuck in circumstances beyond their control.

Trinity's story started before getting his first computer. His mother was thrown out of her home in a rural village because she shamed her parents by becoming pregnant.

The baby's father was not taking responsibility. The shame pushed her to travel to the big city, Kampala, to try to provide for her yet unborn son. Little did she know that there was no one in Kampala for her to rely on, and she ended up in one of the largest slums in the world. On December 25, 1992, Trinity was born.

Trinity's life was never easy. He grew up in one of the worst slums in the world, which is all his mother could afford. His mom took jobs in the slums so she could take her newborn son to work with her. He did not get any formal education, even though his mother wanted that more than anything. When Trinity was nine years old, his mother took a job in the city, so she could no longer look after him nor take him with her. With his newfound situation, Trinity, at just nine years old, joined B13, one of the 30-plus gangs in the slums of Kampala.

Along with his friends, Trinity was taught to loot, steal, beat, and fight on behalf of the gang. They needed to do whatever they could to bring money and favor to their gang leader. From the age of nine until two weeks before his 13th birthday, he was on the streets, fearing for his life every day.

This was his ticket out, for himself, his mom and his little brother.

When the missionaries approached him in early December 2005, Trinity had no idea how his life was about to change. The request for a computer was initially all about escaping into video games, to block out all of the pain that he had lived through. Over the next few years, he started realizing what the computer could do and started to learn about computer graphics, video production, and website development.

When Trinity received the opportunity to do design work for Coca-Cola, his life would never be the same. This was his ticket out, for himself, his mom, and his little brother. Yet, he knew there was something more for him to do, something more important. After nine months of work, Trinity quit his job and went back to the slums, where he knew he was supposed to be doing something more meaningful.

When he returned to the slums, everyone thought he was crazy. How could he give up the golden goose that would allow him to exit such a challenging situation? It was only a few weeks after returning to the slums that he met Megan. Megan was only 16 years old and her father had recently fallen off a ladder and broken his back. As the oldest of six children, Megan was told the best way to support her family was to become a prostitute. She was planning to go out on the street that night and sell her body. It was in this moment that Trinity knew he needed to do something.

He told Megan not to do it and that he would find a way. He decided to teach Megan and one of her friends every-thing he knew about computers. What had taken him two years to learn, Megan learned in three months. He was able to teach her about web development and graphic design.

According to Trinity, Megan is brilliant and someone whom he places deep trust in. So much so that eight years later, she is the COO of his companies. Trinity knows that brilliance is equally distributed … opportunity is not!

All the skills that Trinity developed in those years playing with his computer are now the foundation of the work that his company, *era92,* pursues. Today, *era92* is a collection of companies based in Kampala and focused on impact. The core business is a talent agency, *era92 Group,* that takes on some of the best and brightest students and puts them to work serving clients across the globe. *Era92* also owns a safari company, a car wash, an investment fund, and more. The core offering that started it all is the training program, *era92 Elevate,* which they offer to street kids for free.

The youth are identified by local churches. And *era92 Group* delivers used containers filled with computers to the local slums. There are now six containers in slums across Uganda and one in Kenya. Since 2018, *era92* has trained over 3,500 young people and employs about 120 people. In 2025, they expect to graduate over 2,000 students, and they have created so many jobs. It fills his heart, yet Trinity has only gotten started.

In looking at the dots and connecting them backwards, I went to OC in 2024 to meet Trinity and learned that his businesses are evolving daily. What Trinity is doing is weaving his vision and his skills for the young people of Uganda, and eventually across Africa.

What I Learned from Trinity ...

Trinity is a blessing in my life. He is a special someone who provides me with amazing perspective. I have mentioned many times in this book that our situation in life doesn't determine our joy. Trinity is one of the best examples of this for me. He is a light when he walks into a room, even though he is naturally introverted. His passion for making an impact in the lives of others is what makes him so special. I look forward to sharing his story with the world and helping him make the largest impact possible.

Thank you, Trinity, for knowing what you are, who you are, and why you are here!

9

What's Next?

If knowing what you are, who you are, and why you are is the foundation of joy, where do you go next?

The stories shared in this book have painted my path to joy. The stories about Armstrong and Trinity show me that joy is not determined by your situation in life. Both Armstrong and Trinity, and most of the people that I met in Uganda, walk this planet with joy. They have everything that they need, yet most Westerners would say they have nothing. What I learned is that they might be impoverished, but they are not poor. If anything, I believe that we are poor, at least emotionally and spiritually.

Carrie Rich, as well as many others whom I have met through Opportunity Collaboration, taught me about the importance of work being meaningful. For many, making a living, raising a family, and being kind is enough. For some reason, my DNA does not align with that. For me, I need my work to have meaning. I cannot help people make money so that they can drive a nicer car, buy a bigger house, and not contribute back to the community. That is not in alignment with me. I need to have meaningful work, and what is meaningful to me might not be meaningful to someone else.

All the CAF athletes have taught me so much about my identity and my ego, of facing life head-on and never giving up. I've spent countless hours with Jeff Mata and Joe Delegrave. And recently, I met Moon Tucker. Each of their stories carries a similar message. The more you are attached to your identity and your ego, the further you are from your joy. I have learned that I am not my identity, and I am not my ego. This clarity has been critical for me in finding my joy.

Judith Briles has been there for me for 15 years, and she has taught me so many lessons. She is an expert in her craft. She approaches every day with passion and desire to serve her clients, and she does it until her head hits the pillow. She has lost so much in her life, having lost two of her four children, near-death experiences that I didn't share, and so much more, yet she holds her head high and makes each day the best it can be. Thank you, Judith Briles, for demonstrating perseverance, persistence, and patience, and the will to be the best at your craft.

Finally, to Irving Levin and Stephanie Fowler for demonstrating what is possible when we have enough. There are so many amazing causes, and the one they chose: providing first-time college students with scholarships. This year they will graduate their 1,000th college student. Next year they will provide another 1,000 scholarships, and that will be the level of service moving forward. The lives that they touch are amazing, and I hope I can make such an impact in my lifetime.

So, thank you Armstrong, Carrie, Jeff, Moon, Joe, Judith, Irving, Stephanie, and Trinity for knowing What you are, Who you are, and Why you are here. Your strength is what guides me every day.

After traveling to Africa for a month in 2012, I had the crazy idea to take our kids out of school for an extended period. So, in 2015, we packed up our home, put everything into a couple of PODS, and took off on a trip around the globe.

They were curious about who we were.

We spent six months traveling through Australia, Dubai, Israel, Greece, Turkey, Italy, Germany, Austria, Hungary, Czechoslovakia, Netherlands, Belgium, and France. And during nearly six months, no one asked me what I did for a living ... not once.

The people we met weren't interested in my job or accomplishments. They were curious about who we were. That simple shift left a lasting impression on me. Since returning to San Diego in 2015, that insight has stayed with me and helps guide how I live my life moving forward.

The Joy Molecule: My Final Thoughts

Go back to where this all started—with the idea of a molecule.

In the language of chemistry, a molecule is a union of atoms held together by bonds. These bonds are formed through the sharing or exchange of electrons, the outermost energy carriers that allow atoms to connect. Electrons are not just particles; they are possibilities. They create the potential for relationship, for interaction, for something new to emerge. This scientific truth mirrors something beautifully human: our innate desire to bond, to connect, to be part of something more.

Just as molecules form through shared electrons, human connection forms through shared purpose (C_2P). When individuals come together around a common *Why,* they generate energy: creative, emotional, and even spiritual that strengthens their bonds. This is the essence of the **Joy Molecule,** a model for how you connect and learn to find a deeper sense of fulfillment. At the center of this molecule is the **Joy atom.**

Orbiting this core are three essential elements:

> **What you do.**
> **Who you are.**
> **Why you are here.**

When these elements align, and when they resonate with others who share your purpose, they

What the world needs now isn't more networking, it's more *connecting*.

create a kind of human chemistry. And that chemistry, like in nature, is not random. It is intentional. It is powerful. And to me, it is JOY.

When you lead with only the **What,** you become a walking resume. You list your title, your tasks, and your roles like name tags at a networking event. These conversations might open doors, but they rarely open hearts. They're functional, not foundational. Over time, living only through the What leaves you wondering why you feel so replaceable, like an actor in someone else's script.

When you show up only through the **Who,** your personality, your presence, your values, you might feel more authentic, even vulnerable. You get seen for who you are beneath the surface. But without a shared purpose to steer you, even these beautiful connections can lose direction. They become like campfires that once warmed you but slowly burn out when no one tends to the flame.

Your **Why,** *your purpose,* is what gives your relationships depth and direction. It's what turns ordinary connections into lifelong bonds. But purpose alone, without the grounding of what you do best or the truth of who you are, can lose its impact. When your gifts (What) and your presence

(Who) are aligned with your Why, that's when the bond becomes unshakable. That's when connection becomes something more, something that lasts. That is the power of C_2P.

What the world needs now isn't more networking, it's more *connecting*. Not surface-level, resume-driven interactions, but soul-driven, Why-centered relationships. *The Joy Molecule* is your reminder that you are wired for joy, and joy comes not just from being seen, but from being *aligned*. You come alive when you meet others who reflect your Why back to you, when you find people who believe what you believe and care about what you care about.

As you read this final page, I invite you to reflect:

Are your strongest bonds built around your
What, your *Who,* or your *Why?* And

How might your life shift if you focused on connecting
from your *Why* first?

Because in the end, it's not your resume or even your personality that forges the strongest bonds, it's your shared purpose. That's the atom that activates transformation. It is the bond that enhances joy. That's the magic at the heart of the Joy Molecule.

To a life lived with JOY!

Epilogue and Gratitude
Living Is Giving

How can I write a book about joy without including Joe Sigurdson and the Boys to Men Mentoring community? I met Joe through one of my meditation partners, Jared Wells. It was a September afternoon in 2021, and Jared was attending an event at a surf shop on Morena Blvd in San Diego. The event was for an organization called Boys to Men Mentoring (B2M). At the event, Shaun Thompson, the world champion surfer, was present for a book signing for *The Code: Find Your Next Wave.*

I walked into the event not realizing how that organization was going to change my life. Over the past four years, I have met hundreds of amazing young men and adult mentors. I have built great friendships and been to Legacy Ranch on Mt. Palomar numerous times to take young men through their Rites of Passage ceremony. This organization has shown me what it means to be a man and how to show up for myself and others.

Through the organization, I have met amazing human beings like Attila Tota, who lost his arm to cancer in 2018 and walks on this planet with a sense of peace that is uncommon. I have become great friends with Tam, Franco, Francisco, Tim, Joe, Jose, Rose, Vivian, and so many other great staff members who are making an impact. Thank you all for knowing What you are, Who you are, and Why you are here!

I will be donating 50 percent of the proceeds from this book to B2M and CAF. These two amazing organizations have had a significant impact on my life, and I look forward to giving back in ways that can make a lasting impact on the lives they support.

You can learn more about B2M at:
www.BoysToMen.org

You can learn more about CAF at:
www.ChallengedAthletes.org

About the Author

Larry Kesslin is a storyteller, connector, and guide for those ready to redefine success on their terms. After three decades in business development, entrepreneurship, and personal exploration, Larry now helps individuals and organizations find joy by reconnecting with what truly matters: What they bring to the world, Who they are, and Why they're here.

He is the founder of 5 Dots, a consulting firm that focuses on helping professionals build genuine relationships rooted in purpose, starting with the most important relationship, with yourself. He also leads workshops, retreats, and coaching programs centered around *The Joy Molecule.*

Larry's speaking engagements are known for blending real-life stories of amazing people from around the globe, spiritual insight, and grounded business wisdom. He's been invited to keynote conferences, facilitate leadership retreats, and inspire both young professionals and seasoned executives to shift from striving to being. His message is simple but powerful. Joy is not a destination; joy a way of being.

To inquire about working with Larry or inviting him to speak at your next event, please visit www.5-dots.com. You can also email him at **Larry@5-Dots.com.**

How to Work with Larry

If what you've read in these pages has sparked something in you, if you're curious about what joy means in your own life, or how to bring more meaning and connection into your work, then I'd love to explore that with you.

There are three primary ways I work with people:

Coaching

I work with leaders, entrepreneurs, and individuals who have reached a point of success yet still feel a longing for something deeper. My coaching is centered around *The Joy Molecule* framework—helping you uncover your What (your unique gifts), your Who (your truest self), and your Why (your purpose). Together, we'll identify what truly matters to you and create a path that is both fulfilling and sustainable.

Speaking

I speak to audiences about the pursuit of joy, the power of human connection, and redefining success. My talks bring the concepts of *The Joy Molecule* to life through real stories, simple frameworks, and practical insights that inspire people to think differently about what they do, who they are, and why they do it. Whether it's a corporate gathering, nonprofit event, or community group, I tailor each talk to spark meaningful conversation and action.

Partnerships & Collaboration

Beyond coaching and speaking, I work with organizations and communities to build authentic relationships and create Masterminds that lead to growth, innovation, and impact. If you're seeking to deepen your culture, develop your people, or create opportunities for true connection, there may be meaningful ways we can collaborate.

Next Step

If you'd like to learn more about working together, the best way to start is by reaching out directly:

Email: Larry@LarryKesslin.com

Website: www.5-Dots.com

I look forward to connecting with you, hearing your story, and exploring how we can create something meaningful together.

Your Joy Molecule Journey Starts Here

Remember how Armstrong knew flying was his calling? How Trinity discovered his gift with computers? How Irving found joy in seeing potential in others? Now it's your turn to explore.

The Joy Molecule Assessment is my way of helping you think about your own *What, Who,* and *Why.* It's a collection of questions designed to help you reflect on where you are and where you might want to go.

There are no perfect scores or wrong answers. Just honest questions and space for you to discover what alignment might look like in your own life.

Ready to explore? Scan the QR code and let's continue the conversation.

www.ingramcontent.com/pod-product-compliance
Lightning Source LLC
Chambersburg PA
CBHW070343130626
46556CB00007B/3006